ALONG HADRIAN'S WALL

CONDITIONS OF SALE

ALONG HADRIAN'S WALL

DAVID HARRISON

PAN BOOKS LTD : LONDON

First published 1956 by Cassell & Co Ltd.
This edition published 1973 by Pan Books Ltd,
33 Tothill Street, London, SW1.

ISBN 0 330 23468 4

Printed in Great Britain by
Richard Clay (The Chaucer Press), Ltd, Bungay, Suffolk

IVLIANO OPTIMO MINIMO
MEO KARISSIMO

CONTENTS

LIST OF ILLUSTRATIONS

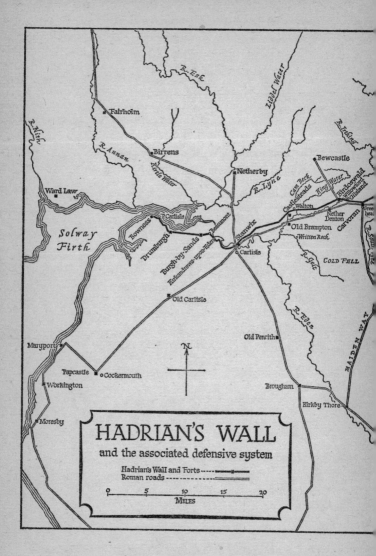

R. Esk

Liddel Water

Fairholm

R. Nith

R. Annan

Birrens

Annan Water

Netherby

R. Lyne

Bewcastle

R. Irding

Ca Beck

King Water

Castlesteads

Birdoswald
Willowford
Gilsland

Walton

Ward Law

Bowness

P. Carlisle

Drumburgh

Burgh-by-Sands

Kirkandrews-upon-Eden

Beaumont

Stanwix

Old Brampton

Nether
Denton

Carvoran

Gree
hea

Solway
Firth

Cartisle

Written Rock

R. Gelt

COLD FELL

R. Eden

Old Carlisle

Old Penrith

MAIDEN WAY

Maryport

N

Tapcastle

Cockermouth

Workington

Brougham

Kirkby Thore

Moresby

HADRIAN'S WALL
and the associated defensive system

Hadrian's Wall and Forts ---- ■
Roman roads -----------------

0   5   10   15   20
MILES

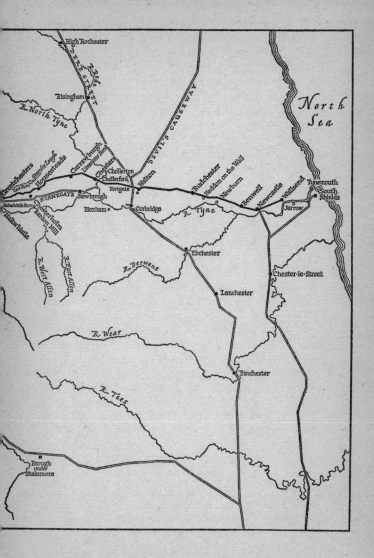

FOREWORD

> Some man or other must present Wall.
> *A Midsummer Night's Dream*, III, i

Let me at the outset disclaim all pretence that there is anything noteworthy in walking the length of the Roman Wall. In these days, when youth is so strenuous and middle age so youthful, seventy-three miles is a trifle. And it has been done before, notably by that hardy antiquary William Hutton, who in 1801, at the age of seventy-eight, not only trudged along the Wall in both directions, but walked there and back from his home in Birmingham, a total of six hundred miles, and all 'to see a shattered wall'. Truly there were giants in those days! And giants are proverbially credited with weak minds.

Yet of the thousands who have visited the Wall and tramped its more attractive sections few, I believe, have troubled to walk its whole length. They probably had more sense. Indeed, the only noteworthy thing about my expedition seems to be its imbecility. And even here old Hutton has set up a record which none will now dare to break.

In 1920 Miss Jessie Mothersole walked the Wall from east to west and recorded her journey in a book adorned with her own paintings. From time to time local societies have organized 'pilgrimages' to the Wall, when those who wished could walk it by stages and be picked up when they had had enough. But it is doubtful how many walked it all, for in 1886 we read that 'Carriages, which may be resorted to at fitting opportunities, will accompany the Pilgrimage throughout ... Those who prefer may walk the whole way and their luggage can be placed in the luggage-cart'. Now that motors have replaced carriages and 'luggage-carts', it is to be feared that the number of 'overall' walkers, if one may use that horrid catchword, has sadly diminished.

If, then, I have joined this select band of imbeciles, I can only plead the urge of that 'wall madness' which has probably attacked more devotees than care to admit it. Having chosen to make a study of Roman Britain, I soon found myself yielding to the lure of those majestic lines of masonry climbing and descending, so daringly and unerringly, the crags of northern Britain. A week at the Summer School of Archaeology at Corbridge in 1953 only whetted my appetite for more. I decided to follow the whole course of the Wall step by step from Wallsend near the mouth of the Tyne to Bowness on Solway Firth, to see for myself all its remaining fragments and those of its auxiliary structures, and thus to obtain a first-hand acquaintance with Hadrian and all his works thereabouts, and those of his successors, such as no reading of archaeological reports could give. Then came the idea of this book, in which I shall try to give my impressions of what I found, in the hope that some who care for the history of our country may be provoked into sampling the attractions of the Wall for themselves.

On reflection, I should like to amend that last sentence. Who am I to expect others to share my enthusiasm? Few people, I believe, are more irritating than those who, having taken up some fad, immediately set out to make converts of the unwilling. 'Let Austin have his swink to him reserved' is my motto, as it was of Chaucer's monk. So, if you don't like my Wall, I shall not greatly mind. I find it fascinating, and I address myself only to those who are prepared to be interested in it too.

I should make it clear that I am no archaeologist, only an amateur historian who knows that he meddles with things under the ground at his peril. But I am writing for those who do not want deep learning but would like to have a

simple account of the Wall – its purpose, its plan, something of its history, and above all the secret, so far as that
can be recovered, of the life and thought of its people. I
shall try, however, to embody the latest findings of the
archaeologists, so far as I can follow them in their difficult
lore.

What, then, is this fascination which Hadrian's Wall
exerts? At best, there are only some miles of masonry, its
upper courses long since removed, a few forts and other
structures in like case, and a number of sites which, however interesting archaeologically, have little to show to the
inexpert visitor. There are far more imposing historical remains scattered throughout Britain – noble cathedrals,
frowning castles, stately mansions, delightful villages, and
even a few walled towns. All these have their lovers, and
rightly so. Yet the Roman Wall is in a class by itself. Not
that it is better than these others, any more than a Haydn
symphony can be called better than a Holbein portrait. But
the Wall is the greatest historical monument in our country
– a magnificent complex of wall, vallum, forts, milecastles,
turrets, supply depots, outposts and roads – bestriding two
counties and linking two seas. The vastness of the conception, and not merely of the work itself, is what rivets the
attention. And there is its history, the history of its making,
its manning, its holding, its loss and recovery, and its final
fate. It has a saga all its own. And a situation and an atmosphere, as I soon discovered for myself. Only Offa's Dyke
can rival it in mere size, and the Dyke has little else.

It is easy to write nonsense about the 'atmosphere' of a
place. But intangibles are often the greatest realities. To
me, at least, every place – every one, that is, which is not
the un-significant product of heartless commercialism –
has its peculiar atmosphere, the sampling of which is one of
the joys of living. It is not merely a question of beautiful
scenery. The South Downs, for example, are not particularly beautiful: but their bare, smooth contours enshrine a
remote, drowsy, immemorial quietness which one would

not have any different, since this is their very essence. You
are not merely content to look at this; you want to soak
yourself in it, to become part of it as you learn to live in it,
and thus to penetrate its secret. So, too, with the mountains
of Snowdonia, where at the right time and place you may
feel yourself lifted up to heaven, only to find hell presently
yawning at your feet. And of course there is the lure of the
sea, as it swirls lazily at the foot of some rocky cliff, redo-
lent of old Celtic legend, whether of Arthurian heroes or of
early saints. And while one is content to take each place as
one finds it, one is always unconsciously searching for the
ideal, like a gourmet delicately appraising his viands and
wines, yet always hoping for perfection, or, more suitably,
like a lover telling over the qualities of his mistresses, yet
always looking for the perfect partner. To me, at least, the
memory of some favourite countryside, suddenly recalled in
all the vividness of its many-sided appeal, can arouse a
homesickness which is almost unbearable. It is this combination of associations which calls one. One's own doings
in that particular piece of country, the feeling of well-being
as one set off on some 'incense-breathing morn', or lit one's
pipe after lunch on some commanding height, the charm of
the natural setting, and the feeling of history all around
which every corner of England fortunately contains – all
these make a Something which has almost a personality of
its own. And all these the Wall has in abundance, as I shall
try to show.

One must admit that the Romans are not everybody's
favourites. They left their mark on history by their achievements, above all in war, statecraft, and jurisprudence. But,
like many successful, practical people, they were rather dull
and unimaginative. They produced some great poetry and
many fine buildings, but here they were mainly standing on
the shoulders of the Greeks. The finest products of the
Greek genius were beyond their grasp and their educational
system aimed chiefly at excellence in rhetoric – eloquent
expression almost regardless of matter. This dislike of

thought endeared them to educated nineteenth-century Englishmen who, drilled in the classics and determined to extract some compensation for their schoolboy drudgery, saw themselves as neo-Romans bursting with *pietas, gravitas* and *simplicitas*.

Yet there was, after all, something fine in the old Roman character – its integrity, its stoic devotion to duty, its cultivation of the homely virtues. Their Empire, it has been said, was built by ordinary men doing extraordinary things. But this was only half the picture. What of the licence of the upper classes who battened on the spoils of empire, of the senseless tyrannies of those sadistic megalomaniacs Caligula, Nero and Domitian, of the almost casual revolutions by murder which disgraced the third century AD? What of slavery, which, however softened in practice, ever lurked as a corroding dehumanizing influence on the whole social system? What of the craze for public shows, with their appalling mass carnage? Some people like to joke about throwing Christians to the lions. These things happened long ago, it is true, but they hurt as much as any Nazi or Bolshevik atrocity of our own time. Under Titus, that most amiable of Emperors, five thousand criminals fought to the death in one day. Claudius ordered gladiators who fell accidentally to be slain, so that he might watch their dying faces, while Nero made forty senators and sixty knights fight in the arena. Even Cicero and the younger Pliny, likewise amiable men, argued that the amphitheatre inculcated contempt of pain and death, while the idle proletariat simply loved it. It is one of the duties of the historian to 'get under the skin' of his subjects, to try and see the world as they saw it: but here he is almost baffled. What are we to make of such a people? Can any good thing, we are tempted to ask, come out of a society so devoid of humanity and moderation?

I must own that I find the people of the Middle Ages far more attractive. As I watch them, after the collapse of the Roman Empire, slowly but hopefully starting to rebuild civilization, setting out on that 'adventure of Europe' which is still our adventure, I feel that these people are doing something of enormous significance. So, too, in the sixteenth century, when new worlds were suddenly opened on all sides, one knows that things are happening which are to affect the lives of all of us now. Compared with these, is not the story of the Roman Empire but an old song, signifying nothing?

This might be true had medieval man been able to make an entirely fresh start. But he could not: he had first to recover as much as he could of the heritage of Rome itself. What we call western civilization is the child of Rome, of that later Empire which embraced within a single political framework all the earlier achievement of western man – the material advances made in Egypt and Mesopotamia, the many-sided culture of the Greeks, the political and legal contribution of Rome herself, and the religious genius of Israel, finding its highest expression in Christianity. Rome has gone, her occupation of Britain was but an episode in our history; but we Europeans are her spiritual heirs, whatever addition we may have made to her legacy. Whoever visits the Wall will see, not a few unmeaning stones, but the outward and visible sign of the power which for the first and only time made the western civilized world one. He will see one of those many frontiers which that power drew between civilization and barbarism. Outside was poor 'unaccommodated man', within reigned that *immensa Romanae pacis maiestas* which conferred such inestimable benefit on millions by its mere unspectacular persistence.

No wonder the Wall has had its lovers. From the sixteenth century, when Englishmen first displayed serious interest in the antiquities of their island, it has exerted an ever-increasing attraction. Unfortunately this interest has barely kept pace with the activity of the vandals who, as security returned to the Borders, have demolished stretch after stretch for building or agriculture. What remains is now happily secure and for the last century archaeologists have been busy forcing the Wall to yield up its secrets. Much yet remains to be done, many sites still await detailed exploration, but at least we now know with fair certainty how and by whom it was built, when it was overrun and by whom it was restored.

That interminable bore, John Leland, mentions the Wall in his *Laborious Journey and Search of John Leland for England's Antiquities given of him as a New Year's Gift to King Henry the VIII*, but his notices are jejune to the point of exasperation. Very different was the work of William Camden, sometime headmaster of Westminster under Elizabeth I, whose massive *Britannia* set forth the topography of the realm with learning and pride. Just before the Queen's death he toured most of the Wall with Robert Cotton, afterwards Sir Robert of the famous manuscripts. 'Verily', he wrote, 'I have seen the tract of it over the high pitches and steep descents of hills, wonderfully rising and falling ... It had many towers and fortresses, about a mile distant from another, which they call castle-steeds, and more within little fenced towns, termed in these days Chesters, the plots or ground works whereof are to be seen in some places four square; also turrets standing between these'. Camden thought that Hadrian was responsible for the Vallum, Severus for the Wall, but nevertheless his was valuable pioneer work. In the early eighteenth century a Presbyterian minister, John Horsley, gave a painstaking account of the Wall in his *Britannia Romana*, and the celebrated antiquary William Stukeley included the Wall in a tour which was recorded much later (1776) in his *Iter Boreale*.

William Hutton, mentioned above, deserves a paragraph to himself, less because of his learning – for he confessed that since the age of six 'the battledore was the last book I used at school' – than for his quaint personality and the sheer absurdity of his madcap exploit, surpassing even that of Will Kemp's dance from London to Norwich two centuries earlier. His daughter Catherine accompanied him as far as the Lakes, riding pillion behind a servant. They worked to a regular routine, he rising at four and walking to the next stage, she following a-horse at seven, in time to join him for breakfast. He then rested two hours and set off again, Catherine overtaking him later and going ahead to bespeak dinner and beds at a convenient inn. He walked the Wall in a black suit, carrying a bag, an umbrella and an inkhorn, garb which earned him several frigid welcomes, the gentry taking him for a 'person employed by Government to examine private property for the advancement of taxation', humbler folk seeing him as a sinister agent of enclosing authorities or rent-raising landlords. At Carrawburgh 'I was treated with great civility, when they found I was neither Exciseman, Spy nor Methodist Preacher'. At times it was so hot, says Catherine, that he actually unbuttoned his waistcoat, and 'his bulk visibly diminished every day'. Nevertheless one pair of shoes sufficed him for the whole six hundred miles and he scarce wore a hole in his socks. He was conscious of his folly, as he called it, and wrote: 'Perhaps I am the first man that ever walked the whole length of this Wall and probably the last that ever will attempt it'. We shall meet his honest but somewhat strait-laced personality again, as we attempt, though not in his sartorial outfit, to follow his steps.

A few years later the historian John Lingard walked the Northumberland section of the Wall and left a manuscript account, quaintly entitled *Mural Tourification*. Apparently 'tourification' was then a new word, which happily did not take root. It was too prophetic of modern monstrosities like 'hospitalization'. Then came the valuable researches of the Reverend John Hodgson, who first challenged the view of Camden and argued that the Wall and the Vallum were alike the work of Hadrian. This theory, now definitely established, was publicized by John Collingwood Bruce, whose *Roman Wall* (1851: third edition, 1867), embodying the valuable excavations of John Clayton of Chesters, became the basis of all later research. It has been kept up to date in form handy for the pocket (last edition 1947, by Professor I. A. Richmond, and so hereinafter referred to, as the lawyers say, as 'Bruce-Richmond'), and was my constant companion – my *Pilgrim's Progress* – throughout my expedition. Since then archaeological research has redoubled its pace, the results being published in *Archaeologia Aeliana* (the journal of the Society of Antiquaries of Newcastle-upon-Tyne), the *Transactions* of the Cumberland and Westmorland Antiquarian and Archaeological Society, the *Journal of Roman Studies*, and elsewhere.

1

THIS MAN HADRIAN

Ego nolo Caesar esse,
ambulare per Britannos.
The poet Florus to the Emperor Hadrian

Before we embark on our 'mural tourification', we had better make the acquaintance of the man but for whom there would have been no Wall to walk along.

Publius Aelius Hadrianus – or, to give him his official title as emperor, IMPERATOR CAESAR TRAIANUS HADRIANUS AUGUSTUS – was born about AD 76 at Italica, near Seville, of Italian stock. He served with distinction in the wars of his kinsman Trajan, won the favour of that Emperor's wife, and married his great-niece. Shortly before his death in 117 the childless Emperor adopted Hadrian as his son (or so it was said), thus ensuring the latter's quiet succession as *princeps* – the disguised autocrat of the Roman world.

Hadrian's character is fascinating in its contradictions. There is no doubt of his capability: in fact, he was one of the most brilliant of the Emperors. He at once reversed Trajan's policy of expansion, which he saw the Empire could not afford, and abandoned that Emperor's annexations beyond the Euphrates. His policy was peace, if possible, but not the peace of sloth. He was *curiositatum omnium explorator*, an investigator of all strange things, and this ingrained curiosity impelled him to make two prodigious tours of the whole Empire. On these he shared the hardships of his legions, often marching twenty miles a day fully armed, and never, we are told, covering his head. His

aim, he often declared, was to rule for the good of his subjects, not his own. Yet he was scarcely a popular ruler,
except with his legions. Though he cared for their comfort,
visiting the sick in their quarters, though he softened the
hard lot of the slaves, though he weeded out corruption in
the administration, he was a severe disciplinarian and employed secret agents to spy out abuses. He encouraged the
extension of Roman life in the provinces, especially by the
founding of new towns, the basis of Roman civilization. He
was generous to his friends: yet he often callously disgraced those whom he had raised in his service, and he
compelled his brother-in-law Servianus to commit suicide
though in his ninetieth year for fear he should survive him
and seize the throne.

His private life was equally enigmatic. He was accused of
immoral relations with women and men, and he certainly
did not hit it off with his wife, Sabina, despite the suggestions to the contrary on his coins. He was a lover of Roman
antiquity and adorned his capital with fine buildings, yet he
revelled in Greek culture. He was an ardent connoisseur in
painting, sculpture and music, wrote erotic verses and an
autobiography which he published under the name of one
of his freedmen. He climbed Aetna and a Syrian mountain
to see the sunrise. It is said that he could write, dictate
orders, listen and chat all at the same time: but this I beg
leave to doubt. Not even Lord Beaverbrook could fill so
many simultaneous rôles. Not the least of his legacies was
the 'wave of beards', as the authors of *1066 And All That*
would call it, which his own, grown to hide some natural
blemish, imposed on Roman fashion.

He had, too, a pretty wit. He often bathed with the
crowd in the public baths, where he once saw one of his
veterans rubbing himself against the wall. When asked
the reason, the man explained that he could not afford a
slave to perform this office for him. Hadrian immediately
gave him some slaves and a fund for their upkeep. On his
next visit he found several old men rubbing themselves

against the wall, but Hadrian refused the bait to his gene-
rosity and ordered them to fall in and rub one another. On
another occasion an elderly man to whom he had refused a
favour presented himself again with his grey hair dyed; but
Hadrian repelled him, saying, 'I have already refused your
father.' When the poet Florus addressed some quipping
verses to him, beginning –

> Caesar I'd not care to be,
> Touring Britain don't suit me,
> I can't stand those Scythian winters, etc,

Hadrian riposted with –

> Florus I'd not care to be,
> Touring taverns on the spree,
> Scrounging in the cookshops likewise,
> Prey to swarms of juicy houseflies.

In his last illness he ordered a servant to kill him, but
Antoninus Pius stopped this. Then he tried to kill himself,
but the dagger was taken from him. Finally he demanded
poison from his physician, who killed himself to avoid
complying. As he lay dying he composed the well-known
verse to his soul –

> Anima vagula blandula,
> hospes comesque corporis,
> quae nunc abibis in loca,
> pallidula frigida nudula?
> nec ut soles dabis iocos?

which Matthew Prior has translated (not too happily) –

> Poor, little, pretty, fluttering thing,
> Must we no longer live together?
> And dost thou prune thy trembling wing,
> To take thy flight thou knowest not whither?

Thy humorous vein, thy pleasing folly,
Lies all neglected, all forgot;
And pensive, wavering, melancholy,
Thou dread'st and hop'st thou know'st not what.

Spartianus, who gives us most of these details in his Life
of Hadrian in the *Historia Augusta* a century and a half
later, sums up his enigmatic personality as composed of
gentle severity, licentious gravity, cautious haste, tight-
fisted liberality, bland deception, savage clemency, *et sem-
per in omnibus varius*. Truly it was no colourless nonentity
who gave Britain her most remarkable historical monument.

At Hadrian's accession Roman Britain was in the throes
of a crisis. It was just under eighty years since the province
had been inaugurated by Claudius. Since then Roman
generals and Roman governors had thoroughly conquered
the lowlands of England and the highlands of Wales, but
the wild mountains of Caledonia presented an apparently
insoluble problem. The famous governor Agricola (AD 78–
85) had indeed made a bold bid to conquer Caledonia. Having subdued the turbulent Brigantes of northern England,
he had built a line of forts from Carlisle to Corbridge (and
possibly farther eastwards, though of this we have no posi-
tive evidence yet), along the road later known as the Stanegate. From these as a base he had then pushed into the
heart of Caledonia, consolidating his advance by further
forts, and had routed its natives at Mons Graupius, only to
be recalled the following year.

I have referred to north Britain as Caledonia, not Scotland. There is a popular idea, derived from their later on-
slaughts on Roman Britain, that the North was always
peopled by Picts and Scots. But the Scots, of course, were
Irishmen, who did not begin to migrate to western Scotland
in serious numbers till the fifth century, while the Picts are
first mentioned in 297. Meanwhile the peoples of what is
now Scotland were referred to by classical writers under a

number of names, doubtless representing different tribal
units. They were all Celts, like the Britons farther south,
and 'Picts', when it does appear, is generally taken to mean
the 'painted men', applied to one of these tribes which may
have become the ruling power. The whole subject is contro-
versial and it is best to call all these peoples Caledonians
for the present.

Let us see exactly what was the problem that confronted
the imperial government at this stage. Unless the highlands
of Britain were firmly held the valuable lowlands – where
Roman towns, linked by magnificent roads, Roman industries and commerce, and Roman life in all its budding
novelty were now flourishing – could never be secure. Yet
the highlands were worthless in themselves and expensive
to subdue and retain. Three legions were required to hold
England and Wales, and they were admirably placed – the
Second at Caerleon-on-Usk, the Twentieth at Chester and
the Ninth at York, all large strong fortresses. With a fourth
legion permanently stationed near the Forth, it should have
been possible to hold Caledonia without troubling to subdue it thoroughly. A punitive expedition every time rebellion raised its head would have done the job. But it was just
this fourth legion that the Empire could not spare. There
had indeed been four legions in Britain for a time, but just
after Agricola's recall it had been necessary to transfer one
to Germany. *Hinc illae lacrimae.*

For at some time in the second decade of the second
century a great revolt in the north of the province annihilated the Ninth Legion. An inscription of 108 is our last
record of its existence. Thereafter it disappears from history and was never reconstituted (on my return from my
little expedition I heard that some wit among my friends
had spread the rumour that I had at last found this lost
legion and been conscribed into its ranks. This, like the
report of Mark Twain's death, was greatly exaggerated).

It is a pity that we are not better informed of this
disaster, for then we could attempt some estimate of Had-

rian's statesmanship in deciding to cut his losses and keep
out the enemy by his famous Wall. All we have is two
cryptic sentences. Fronto mentions in an aside the slaughter
of Roman soldiers at the hands of Britons at the time of
Hadrian's accession: while Spartianus merely says that
'Having restored the army's morale, he crossed to Britain,
where he set many things to rights and built a wall eighty
miles long to separate the Romans from the barbarians.'

These chance statements must conceal a deal of anxious
conference at imperial headquarters. We have to remember
that Britain was not the only morsel on Hadrian's plate. It
was 122, or perhaps 121, when he visited Britain. He had
already been to Gaul and Germany: he was to go on to
Spain, to Africa and then to the East, where Trajan's in-
volvements must somehow be straightened out. Clearly he
decided that it was no time to renew Agricola's forward
policy. That governor's last conquests in Caledonia had
recently been overrun by the barbarians. Hadrian decided
that Caledonia must be abandoned and that a new frontier
must be drawn and defended by stone and soldiers so that
the barbarians could never again penetrate the peaceful
south. This was no desperate Maginot Line expedient. In
the then state of military science such a fortified frontier, or
limes, was the best defence possible. It had already proved
its worth in Germany. And fortunately the frontier then
held coincided fairly accurately with the ideal position for
such a *limes*. There was in fact no real alternative. A line
from the mouth of the Tyne to Solway Firth was the
shortest across Britain that could not be outflanked (except
by sea, and that could be provided against): it was acces-
sible from the legionary bases at York and Chester by good
and not too long roads: and the valleys of the Tyne, the
Irthing and the Eden enabled it to be driven across not too
difficult country. And where, in the central sector, the going
was difficult, the crags and hills could be made to assist,
rather than impede, the defences.

So orders were given and the Wall arose.

2

THE BUILDERS

Exegi monumentum aere perennius.
HORACE, Odes, III, XXX, I

We've got to fix this thing for good an' all;
It's no use buildin' wat's a-goin' to fall.
J. R. LOWELL

At this stage I can imagine some readers exclaiming:
'Good heavens, when is this man going to stop talking and
start walking?' But patience, *bone lector*. Consider that
when we do start walking we shall encounter such fearsome
things as milecastles, turrets, praetoria, and what not, not
to mention that enigma, the Vallum. It will be difficult to
explain all these *ambulando*. Besides, unless we get a preliminary picture of the whole works – in the literal sense of
that phrase – we shall miss the very essence of the Wall
itself. But I shall try to be brief. Those readers who are well
informed on these matters can skip this chapter.

Hadrian entrusted the job of building the Wall to his
lieutenant, the governor of Britain, Aulus Platorius Nepos.
No doubt the imperial engineering department soon had a
blue-print of the proposed works ready. But the Romans
were practical people. They were not going to put it into
execution regardless of hard fact: if they encountered the
unexpected as the work proceeded, they were quite willing
to modify their plans in detail. They did, in fact, find many
surprises and changed their minds accordingly. Hence the
bewildering afterthoughts which have baffled antiquaries
for so long and have only recently yielded up their secrets.

I have talked of the Wall, but that is only part of the

story. Hadrian's work is best seen as a huge defensive complex, including forts for a holding garrison and a wall with strong points at regular intervals for a patrolling garrison. Agricola's forts on the Stanegate would do for the first, so Nepos at once set his men to work on the Wall itself. He employed detachments from all three legions – for the legionaries were used to this sort of work and always carried entrenching and engineering tools – with some help from the fleet and auxiliary troops. We know this because the builders 'signed their names' to their work by inscriptions recording the sections done by a legion, a cohort or a century. 'Centurial stones' placed at the end of the section, about forty-five yards, allotted to a century, are common and generally give the name of the centurion in charge. The stones for the Wall were quarried from conveniently near quarries, many of which can still be identified. Its facing stones were of regular shape, about ten by six inches, often tapering as much as twenty inches into the core of the wall, which was poured around them to give solidarity. The legionaries appear to have been divided into gangs, each working from the east westwards. First the ditch which was to front the Wall on the north was dug. Then the foundation of the Wall was built as far as the River Irthing. Next, one gang erected the milecastles and turrets in their appropriate positions, while another completed the superstructure of the wall. Naturally, the former soon outstripped the latter.

The Wall was planned to be ten Roman feet (each of 11·7 inches) wide, but when the whole wall on this scale had been built from Newcastle to near Brunton and a foundation of this width carried westwards from Brunton to the River Irthing, it was decided to finish the work on a narrower gauge of eight Roman feet. In western Northumberland, therefore, the Wall is narrow on a broad foundation. It was also decided to extend the Wall eastwards to Wallsend, on which sector it is therefore narrow throughout. The core of the broad wall, incidentally, was composed of

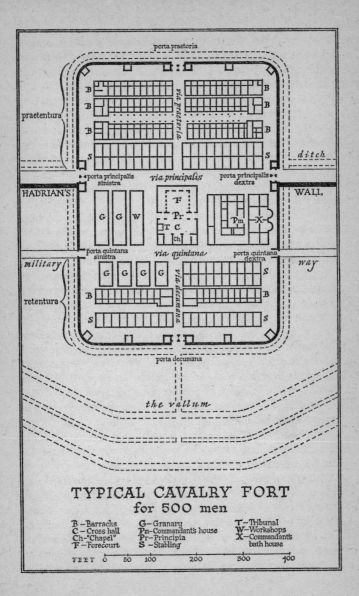

TYPICAL CAVALRY FORT
for 500 men

B – Barracks   G – Granary   T – Tribunal
C – Cross hall   Pm – Commandant's house   W – Workshops
Ch – "Chapel"   Pr – Principia   X – Commandant's
F – Forecourt   S – Stabling   bath house

FEET   0   50   100   200   300   400

rubble and clay, that of the narrow wall of rubble and mortar made of limestone, sand and gravel. Possibly orders came to economize on building and it was then found that a narrow wall with a clay and rubble core would shift slightly and therefore limestone was employed. Possibly there was faulty staff-work or some 'brass-hat' blundered: but in the absence of definite evidence it seems kinder to assume that the engineers had a reason for these mysterious changes of plan. In Cumberland, where limestone was unobtainable, the Wall was built of turf, twenty feet wide, but this was gradually replaced, as opportunity allowed, by a stone wall nine Roman feet wide.

All these rather dry details, and much more, have been wrested from the structure by patient research, but no research can give us the exact height of the Wall, which nowhere stands in its original grandeur. Old observers vary in their statements of the height of the remains they saw, but the latest estimates suggest that it was originally about fifteen feet high, with a parapet of about six feet above that, a total of perhaps twenty-one feet. Its length, as everyone knows, was eighty Roman, or seventy-three and a half English miles from Wallsend to Bowness. Along its front, about twenty feet to the north (or six feet where the Wall was of turf), ran a broad deep ditch, except where crags or seashore rendered this extra defence unnecessary.

A legion, by the way, consisted in Hadrian's day of five to six thousand heavy infantry, divided into ten cohorts and sixty centuries, with a small cavalry detachment of about one hundred and twenty men. It was commanded by a general of senatorial rank, under whom served six tribunes and sixty centurions. At that time the legionaires were all Roman citizens and were mostly provincials, not Italians. The inferior auxiliary troops were levied from the subject races of the remoter provinces and at first only became eligible for citizenship on discharge. They were officered by Romans of lower than senatorial rank and consisted of both cavalry and infantry units. The legionaries fought with a throwing-spear, a short sword and a dagger; they carried a cylindrical shield and wore a metal cuirass over a leather tunic, and boots. The auxiliaries carried a longer thrusting-spear and a long sword, but would often fight with the weapons native to the district whence they were recruited. Both legionaries and auxiliaries served, at this period, for twenty-five years. All these arrangements were radically modified about the end of the third century, when the army was reorganized to meet new situations. Greater use was made of cavalry, more barbarian troops were employed, and before the Western Empire fell the army had been almost completely barbarized.

As the Wall was a-building, it was furnished with mile-castles and turrets. Milecastles were very small rectangular forts, generally some forty to sixty feet broad and sixty-five to seventy-five feet long internally, placed at intervals of about a Roman mile all along the Wall, which formed their north front. Each had north and south gates, and accommodation for thirty to fifty men in one or two barrack blocks, together with an oven. On the turf Wall they were built of turf, with timber buildings and gateways: elsewhere of stone. Some milecastles have their long sides north to south, others east to west: there are also differences in the planning of their gateways, reflecting building by different gangs. Between each pair of milecastles were two turrets, at equal distances, each about fourteen feet square, built of stone, even in the turf Wall. Where the Wall is narrow on a broad foundation the north Wall has been built to the broad gauge at milecastles and turrets and for a short stretch on each side of them, showing that the building gangs had been sent on ahead to erect them, leaving the wall-builders to catch up later.

By means of detachments stationed in the milecastles, from which smaller parties would be sent out to the turrets and relieved at intervals, the whole length of the Wall could be easily kept under observation and any attack immediately notified by signal.

Yet before the Wall was finished it was decided to re-inforce it by placing forts along its course. We know this because in some cases a milecastle, a turret or the ditch of the Wall itself has been replaced by a fort, yet inscriptions show that many of the forts were built under Platorius Nepos. Clearly it was found that to rely on Agricola's Stanegate forts would not give security. Whether the Cale-donians threatened a mass attack, whether the Brigantes resented the driving of this mighty work through their ter-ritory (which extended at least into south-west Scotland) we may never know. Opposition of some kind there clearly was; this is suggested also by Hadrian's sending one of his ablest generals, Julius Severus, to Britain about 130. So the authorities decided to take no risks. To the patrolling gar-rison on the Wall, operating from milecastles and turrets, was now added a fighting garrison, no longer lodged on the Stanegate, but brought up to the Wall likewise.

These forts (*castella*) are the *foci* of interest as we tour the Wall. Though built to a general plan, based on the tem-porary 'marching camps' of earth which the legions always threw up when they halted for the night on campaign, they varied in size from nine to two acres and the diversity of their situation gives each something of a separate indi-viduality. All were rectangular, with rounded corners, and were protected by a stone wall some five feet thick and an external ditch, the earth from which was piled up against their walls within. Most of the earliest forts projected be-yond the Wall and had six gates, one double gate on each side and a single gate as well on the longer sides, which lay at right angles to the Wall. The north and the main east and west gates lay north of the latter. This arrangement enabled the garrison to deploy rapidly and, with similar sorties from the north gates of the milecastles, to roll up the enemy against the Wall. We must not imagine the Romans fighting upon the Wall, which, in R. G. Collingwood's words, was only 'an elevated sentry walk'.

Joining the gates were four main roads within the fort.

The *via principalis* linked the main side gates, the *via praetoria* joined this and the front gate; the *via quintana* ran parallel to and at the rear of the principal road; and the *via decumana* joined the *via quintana* and the rear gate. At the junction of the *viae principalis* and *praetoria* stood the headquarters building (*principia*), containing a forecourt adorned with colonnades, a central covered hall and a rear block of five rooms. The middle room was the 'chapel' (*sacellum*), dedicated to the worship of the Emperor and containing his statue, the standards of the regiment and perhaps images of Jupiter and Mars. Under it might be a strong room, where the regimental pay and the soldiers' savings were kept. The other rooms housed the administrative staff, without which no Roman, any more than any modern, army was complete. In one corner of the cross-hall was a dais, from which the commandant administered discipline to defaulters.

Next to the headquarters stood the commandant's house (*praetorium*), often supplied with baths and central heating. 'Praetorium' was used also for a general's quarters or for any building reserved for official use, as readers of St Mark's Gospel may remember. The remainder of the fort was occupied by barracks for the troops, quarters for junior officers, granaries built on raised floors for protection against damp, stables where the garrison was horsed, and miscellaneous buildings such as workshops. The gateways of forts and milecastles were built in longer and often massive stones. The walls of the forts were furnished with stout towers at their angles and gateways, and often at intervals between, which must have given the whole structure an impressive appearance of strength.

Outside the fort was the regimental bath-house. Here, too, as time went on, grew up a native village (*vicus*), peopled at first by camp-followers, then by time-expired veterans and their families, and often growing into small but flourishing communities of stone houses or huts, with temples, taverns and shops, whose inhabitants tilled the surrounding fields and carried on a brisk but exiguous trade. Few of these, except at Housesteads, have been excavated, but their extensive nature has recently been revealed by air-photography. Here the troops found such recreation as their leisure and the north-British climate allowed. From the time of Severus they were permitted to live out of camp. These villages were undefended, a testimony to the general security, though in the last years of Roman occupation some of their inhabitants may have found refuge within the forts.

Platorius Nepos seems to have built the Wall, with its milecastles and turrets, and about ten forts, before his term as governor expired about 126. To have accomplished all this in about five years was a remarkable feat. Under his successor or successors a few further forts were added, including Wallsend, Carrawburgh, Greatchesters and Carvoran, to fill gaps which had proved awkward in practice. This made a total of sixteen forts, if we include Drumburgh, which is more like a large milecastle.

All this does not complete the tale of the wall complex. To the south of the Wall, except between Wallsend and Newcastle, was built an earthwork, miscalled the Vallum since Bede's day. This was a ditch ten feet deep and twenty feet wide, with a flat bottom eight feet wide. The excavated soil was piled up in two mounds, each twenty feet wide, on the banks, about thirty feet north and south of the edge of the ditch, the whole system thus making an intricate obstacle some one hundred and twenty feet wide. Unlike the Wall, which always seeks the highest ground, the Vallum aims at directness and runs in a series of straight lines at distances varying from a few yards to half a mile from the Wall. Its purpose has aroused much speculation. It was clearly not for defence, and appears to have been intended to mark the boundary between the military and civil zones, to keep out intruders from the south from the defences and to enable the milecastle garrisons to patrol their rear. Professor I. A. Richmond defines it as 'the rearward patrolled boundary of the military zone associated with the Wall'. For at the forts it was crossed by a causeway carrying a road and a large gateway, while at the milecastles the roads cut its northern mound only, allowing the garrison to patrol the Vallum but preventing civilians from entering.

When the Vallum approaches a fort, it generally deviates to the south, showing that it was a later work. But other evidence shows that it was constructed not later than the narrow Wall, perhaps by the immediate successor of Nepos, that is, before 130. Thus at Carrawburgh the fort, which is either contemporary with, or additional to, the narrow wall, was built over the Vallum, while at Birdoswald wooden shacks were built on the Vallum and were destroyed when the ditch for the stone fort was dug. The fact, too, that no Vallum was added east of Newcastle suggests that it was elsewhere completed before the narrow Wall. We must therefore envisage all these works going forward almost contemporaneously amidst considerable changes in plan. I cannot avoid the impression that here at least there was considerable confusion in the planners' minds. At any rate, when, less than twenty years later, as a result of a renewed Roman advance, the Antonine Wall was built from Forth to Clyde and the garrison on Hadrian's Wall reduced, the Vallum was deliberately defaced. At intervals of forty-five yards it was broken by crossings made by digging gaps in its mounds and building corresponding causeways across its ditch. This, at least, seems a prodigious waste of effort; and somewhat later, when Caledonia was lost for good, the ditch was recut and many of the causeways removed. Later still, the ditch was again cleaned in places and the débris piled up on its lip to form the 'marginal mound'. We may remember that the troops were not always fighting and that in the intervals occupation had to be found for them, as for National Service men in our own day.

At some time after Wall and forts were completed, the latter were linked by a metalled road, generally called the

Military Way, about twenty feet wide, with paths running
up to each milecastle and turret.

To complete the system, a series of forts, fortlets and
turrets was added along the north Cumberland coast, to
prevent the outflanking of the Wall by boats crossing Solway Firth, and outpost forts were erected at Birrens near
Ecclefechan, at Netherby on the Esk and at Bewcastle six
miles in front of Birdoswald, to protect the Cumberland
portion of the Wall which, owing to the hills to its north,
was 'blind'.

When all these vast works were completed the legions
returned to their three fortresses farther south and the
permanent defence of the northern barrier was entrusted to
auxiliaries. Each fort had a separate regiment allotted to it,
and the variety of these garrisons attests the multitude of
different peoples embraced within the Empire. Gauls, Germans, Netherlanders, Spaniards and Illyrians jostled in
queer proximity along the Wall. At first auxiliaries often
served in provinces distant from their homes, and only one
Wall fort, Newcastle, was garrisoned by a British unit. On
the other hand, British auxiliary regiments are found serving in Germany and eastern Europe from an early date.
Though many of the garrisons were changed during the
long period of Roman rule, some of these served a remark-
ably long time at one station. But it is unlikely that each
unit was solely maintained from its original source, though
it kept its old name. In any case, as the soldiers tended to
marry local women and as their sons generally entered their
fathers' regiments, the latter must have gradually become
more and more British in blood.

The infantry auxiliary units were called cohorts, the
cavalry *alae* (literally 'wings'). Both might comprise either
one thousand or five hundred men nominal, called milliary
and quingenary detachments respectively. *Alae* and quingenary cohorts were commanded by prefects, the larger
cohorts by tribunes. These were all equestrian (knightly)
posts. The usual, but by no means universal, procedure was

for a man who had become a magistrate in his home town to be appointed prefect of a cohort, then a tribune with a legion, and then prefect of an *ala*. If he distinguished himself in this military service, he might then become a 'higher civil servant' in the imperial administration. Cohorts were divided into ten or six centuries, according as they were large or small, cavalry regiments into twenty-four or sixteen *turmae* of about thirty men each, commanded by decurions. While the commanders were generally appointed from outside, the centurions and decurions normally came from the ranks. There would be several NCO's (*principales*), including a standard-bearer, an *optio* or deputy to the centurion, and an armourer. There might also be a regimental doctor, though often the sick and wounded had to rely on some colleague with knowledge of first-aid.

The Corbridge Lion

The troops were housed in long barrack-blocks, each holding one century or two *turmae*. Each block was divided into eight to ten rooms (*contubernia*), each holding eight men, while the officers and NCO's occupied larger rooms at the end of the block. In cavalry forts there were separate stable-blocks divided into compartments for six or seven horses each. Both barracks and stables were often built in double parallel blocks under one roof.

The auxiliary regiments appear to have been assisted by irregular units, referred to as a *numerus* if infantry and a *cuneus* if cavalry; and it has been suggested that these were entrusted with the milecastles and turrets. At all events, it is clear that the Wall complex demanded an enormous force for its manning, probably fifteen to sixteen thousand men in all, or nearly one-third of the total garrison of the whole of Britain.

3

NEWCASTLE-UPON-TYNE AND SOUTH SHIELDS

What mean these stones?
Joshua, iv. 21

Away with him, away with him, he speaks Latin.
2 Henry VI, iv, vii

As the time for my expedition drew near, its folly became daily more apparent. The weather, in that worst of summers for fifty years, grew progressively wetter and colder and blacker until one might have been living in the inside of an egg. I almost postponed my departure, until I reflected that there was no guarantee of an improvement. And I seemed justified when by an apparent miracle Monday the 14th June dawned fair and almost warm.

I had decided to spend my first day in Newcastle and South Shields, visiting the Black Gate Museum in the former and the fort and museum in the latter. The first was an essential preliminary to the walking of the Wall, which I would then start the following day. Tuesday, therefore, saw me on my way to the city centre, but alas! yesterday's weather had deserted me. For twelve long hours the rain streamed down. Newcastle will stand comparison with most other cities for stately buildings, fine shops and other amenities; but under the lowering clouds it was like some city of dreadful night. I thought I might appropriately start my pilgrimage by a visit to the Cathedral Church of St Nicholas, but I had no time to explore its treasures. I stopped only to find the fine marble monument to that

father of scientific study of Hadrian's Wall, John Collingwood Bruce, and to note the inscription –

IN MEMORIAM
JOHANNIS COLLINGWOOD BRUCE LL.D., D.C.L.
VIRI AMABILIS CIVIS OPTIMI EGREGII IUVENUM PRAECEPTORIS
STRENUI RERUM ANTIQUARUM INDAGATORIS ATQUE INTERPRETIS ET
AUCTORUM PRAESERTIM QUI HISTORIAM VALLI ROMANI TRACTAVERUNT
INTER PRIMOS HABITI IDEM CHRISTI FIDELIS DISCIPULUS SUI
PIETATEM OMNIBUS BENEVOLENTIAM PAUPERIBUS ATQUE
AEGROTIS AUXILIUM DILIGENTISSIME
PRAESTABAT
NAT. MDCCCV
OB.
MDCCCXCII

Then I made my way to the Black Gate Museum, which
houses the Roman monuments belonging to the Society of
Antiquaries of Newcastle-upon-Tyne – the largest and best
collection in Britain. Here I was welcomed by the Curator,
Mr T. Arthur Lewis, who not only placed himself at my
disposal for the morning but insisted on giving me lunch at
his club. The Black Gate was the main entrance, added by
Henry III, to Henry II's castle, from which it is now separated by the railway. It is said to take its name from a
seventeenth-century tenant and not from its grimy appearance. Here are numerous objects from the Wall and neighbouring sites, among them a bronze cheek-piece from a
helmet, on which are engraved a woman leading a horse, a
steelyard constructed on the same principle as that now
used, a fine bronze colander, the sole of a child's shoe, the
hoard of coins from Coventina's Well at Carrawburgh and
numerous brooches, including a replica of that famous one
from Greatchesters, product of the Celtic genius which
somehow persisted in the north for some time after the
Roman advent. The original is kept in the bank since its
theft and fortunate recovery. It is very beautiful, but Sir
Arthur Evans surely exaggerated when he called it the
finest creation of antique art. Another copy is on view in
the British Museum.

The principal items in this collection are the inscribed and sculptured monuments. We must remember that in Roman days, before printing, inscriptions in stone were a major means of publicity. And fortunately they are extremely durable. They are, in fact, our chief source, not only for the history of the Roman Empire, but for our knowledge of its social life. In the words of the late R. G. Collingwood, this collection forms 'a library of unique historical documents' and with a little imagination they can recreate for us much of the life of soldiers and civilians who occupied themselves along the Wall.

Cutting inscriptions in stone is a laborious business. Hence the Romans employed considerable abbreviation – almost a kind of shorthand, except that they did not stick to any set rules. It was they who started that passion for initials which has re-appeared like a rash in our time, as in NATO and so many others. Thus 'IOM' at the top of a religious inscription shows that it was dedicated to Jupiter, Best and Greatest (*Iovi Optimo Maximo*). 'VSLM' at the end of such stands for *votum solvit libens merito*, indicating that the donor willingly pays his vow to the deserving power. The three legions are represented by 'LEG II AUG P F', the Second August, Dutiful and Faithful Legion, 'LEG VI VIC' for the Sixth Victorious, and 'LEG XX V V' for the Twentieth Valerian Victorious Legion (after Augustus' general Valerius Messalinus), giving them their full titles conferred for prowess in particular engagements. 'LEG PR PR' stands for *Legatus pro praetore*, the title of the governor of Britain. A 'C' written backwards indicates a centurion or his century. Inscriptions on tombstones commonly start with 'DM', short for *Dis manibus*, originally a reference to the gods of the underworld, but meaning merely 'To the divine shades', that is, 'In memory of'. This was used even for Christians for some time, but with the cessation of Roman rule was replaced by *Hic jacit*. Experts can often date an inscription, within limits, by the style of lettering. Much depends, however, on the cutter. Many inscriptions on the Wall were executed by humble folk, often by common soldiers, and in such cases were not remarkable for elegance. Some of them offend by ending a line minus the last letter of a word, which has perforce to start the following line in ridiculous isolation.

Unfortunately I found that these inscriptions were in course of removal to a temporary museum at 11 Sydenham Terrace, where future visitors will be able to see them all: in due course they will be rehoused at King's College. But with the aid of Collingwood's Guide I was able to pick out the highlights of the collection. From them it is possible to trace much of the history of the Wall. Thus two fine altars, one to Neptune and the other to Oceanus, dredged up from the Tyne while building the Swing Bridge, were set up by the Sixth Legion as thank-offerings for their safe arrival from Germany at Hadrian's orders to replace the unfortunate Ninth. A slab from Milking Gap proves the building of the Wall with its milecastles and turrets under Platorius Nepos. A fragment of a 'war memorial', once built into St Paul's Church, Jarrow, of which another part is in the British Museum, shows us Hadrian praising his troops for repelling the barbarians, recovering Britain and securing it by an eighty-mile barrier from sea to sea.

Next, a beautifully-lettered slab, found in the Tyne, records that about 158, when Julius Verus was governor, Antoninus Pius sent reinforcements from Germany. Clearly that Emperor's recovery of the Scottish lowlands had been followed by a great revolt, in which the legions had suffered considerable losses. The Antonine Wall was finally lost, some time after 180, under Commodus, but Hadrian's defences survived till in 196 the governor of Britain, D. Clodius Albinus, aiming at the Empire, took all the troops he could collect to Gaul. The Caledonians seized the chance to avenge themselves on the power which had so cruelly punished them. Surging over the undermanned Wall, they methodically destroyed it, and all behind up to and including the great fortress at York. There are no records at Newcastle of this destruction but several inscriptions mark the rebuilding by Septimius Severus and his successors.

For the sake of clarity when we come to individual forts, it should be emphasized that this year 197 is one of the crucial dates in the history of the Wall. The second is just a century later, 296, when the Wall was again overrun because the usurper Allectus had withdrawn its garrison. This second destruction was repaired by Constantius Chlorus, father of the Emperor Constantine the Great. The third important date is 367, when Picts, Scots and Saxons united to overwhelm the Wall and devastate all Britain. Roman rule was restored by Count Theodosius, who repaired the Wall for the last time. The fourth date is 383, when Magnus Maximus repeated Albinus' exploit, at some time after which the Wall was finally abandoned.

Tombstones, in spite of their associations, are generally interesting and there are several at Newcastle that repay attention. From Carvoran came a memorial set up by a centurion to his blessed (*sanctissima*) wife, who lived thirty-three years without blemish. This, and others to children, show family affection, and the sadness of early death, as strong then as now. There is a tombstone to a surgeon (*medicus*) serving in the ranks, and another from Halton to a well-deserving slave, erected by his *collegium*. These associations combined the functions of religious fraternities, craft guilds and burial clubs. Some were exclusively for slaves, others included slaves and freedmen, and even free men. We have no knowledge to what extent slavery existed in Roman Britain, but it has left few traces round about the Wall.

All these were memorials and nothing more. There is little to indicate in what state the mourners assumed their departed to be, no expression of a hope of reunion. They seem to say with Catullus

> Nobis cum semel occidit brevis lux
> Nox est perpetua una dormienda.

There are in fact two tombstones praying 'Earth, sit lightly on him,' but this is a mere formality. There is also a fragment of a poem from Risingham apparently containing some prayer for the welfare of the departed soul. Roman ideas on the after-life, if any, were in fact confused. Virgil shows some conception of rewards and punishments, but to him the dead mostly live a shadowy existence in gloom until they return to earth in a new incarnation. Some cults taught that death reunited the soul with the universal spirit, but before the triumph of Christianity there seems to have been a movement towards belief in individual immortality. We shall presently meet a tombstone representing the departed tasting the joys of the garden of paradise. But such memorials are rare in these parts. Most of them are content with a bare 'In memory of', as if their sole concern was to achieve some sort of immortality in the memory of posterity. This brings us to the subject of Roman religion.

In the earliest form it was concerned to procure the benefits of divine power (*numen*) for the individual and the state in a primitive farming community. It had no ethical character: one performed the prescribed rites and the gods, of whom there were a perfect multitude, each presiding over some small activity of mankind or nature, were expected to fulfil their side of the bargain. As the Republic expanded, Greek mythology was adopted and its deities equated with those of Rome. Unfortunately they were already discredited in their homeland and by the end of the Republic Rome was spiritually bankrupt. Her gods, to the upper classes, were little more than a literary convention, though they still had genuine believers among the masses and Augustus inaugurated a revival. We find inscriptions dedicated to Jupiter, Mars, Mercury, Neptune and Apollo from the Wall area. These cults may be called official, but there are also dedications to abstractions like Fortune, Victory, Health and even Nemesis. They must have been rather cold and comfortless, though possibly soldiers and sailors got some sort of a 'kick' out of their trust in Mars or Neptune.

To fill this religious vacuum the cult of the deified Emperor was established. This conception, so difficult for us to grasp, was not oriental but Greek – the idea that supermen were admitted into the society of the gods at death as a reward for their benefits to mankind; an idea not impossible when the gods themselves were conceived as a sort of immortal humans. It was, in fact, a form of patriotic sentiment, called forth by the need to personify and sanctify the State. It was their refusal to sacrifice to the Emperor, thus confessing their apparent disloyalty, that led to the persecution of the early Christians. We find here two altars from Housesteads to Jupiter and the Deities (*numinibus*) of the Emperors.

All these were not religion, as we understand it. Faced with their comparative unreality, many Romans turned to philosophy, others to magic and astrology. Others, again, embraced the 'mystery religions' of the East, whether of Cybele (the Great Mother), of Isis, Astarte or of Mithras, which differed fundamentally from Graeco-Roman religion. Though founded on primitive myths, they were religions of redemption from sin, promising salvation through sacramental rites, and so were capable of refinement into true spirituality. We shall meet them presently as we journey along the Wall.

These cults, though brought to Britain by the Romans, were only accepted by the natives in so far as the latter became romanized in other respects. But the Romans, with their tolerance of all beliefs which they did not consider anti-social, like Druidism and Christianity, adopted many native cults, often equating them with their own. The troops seem to have had a flair for finding out the local godlings and taking them to their hearts, as we shall see. We are left to speculate what these deities meant to their adherents, one hesitates to call them worshippers. As the inscriptions generally record only the paying of a vow, one gets the impression that they meant little more than an insurance against calamity. True religion, affecting the

conduct of men, offering some explanation of the universe
and the purpose of life, and giving them communion with
the Unseen, was to come from the mystery religions and
from that lowly society which, when the Wall was building,
was only just emerging from the catacombs.

The Castle, it may be noted, was tenanted in 1782 by one
Turner, who advertised it as suitable for the erection of a
windmill for grinding corn or making oil: or, as it contained a good spring of water, it was 'a very eligible situation for a brewery'. A few years later the ground floor was
used as a beer cellar, a confectioner had established an ice-
house on its west side and a currier had filled the rest with
workshops. The walls on its top had been planted with cab-
bages and other vegetables, but the surroundings were filled
with pigsties and dunghills. It seems as if the city has been
lucky to secure the Castle's preservation, but in 1809 they
bought it from Turner for six hundred guineas.

The visitor to Newcastle who is interested in the Wall
should not fail to call at 11 Sydenham Terrace, where, in
addition to the inscriptions transferred from the Black
Gate, he will find some excellent models of the milecastles
and turrets of the stone and turf Walls by Mr William
Bulmer, honorary curator to the Society of Antiquaries of
Newcastle. These give a better impression than any picture
of these structures as they were when first built. The milecastles look brave with towers over their north gates and
steps leading up to the parapet walk. But the highlight of
this exhibition is Mr Bulmer's relief model of the whole
Wall. Built on a scale of six inches to one mile, it extends to
no less than forty-seven feet and gives a unique view of the
whole of the Roman works and of the surrounding countryside. It shows, in particular, how the Roman engineers
made the most of natural features in planning their great
defensive barrier. A call should also be made at the Laing
Art Gallery, where are two wallfuls of water colours by
Henry Burdon Richardson, with a few by his brother
Charles, of numerous points along the Wall. These were

specially sketched, and afterwards coloured, by the brothers in 1848 for the first edition of Bruce's *Handbook*, the three enthusiasts touring the Wall together. Besides being works of art, they preserve for us much that has since been obliterated by so-called development.

In the afternoon, if one could call it such, for the rain was even worse and wetter, and the sky blacker, than before, I took the bus to Wallsend, where, in the park, two fragments of Wall and fort have been set up. I then crossed the Tyne to South Shields by the ferry in more than Stygian gloom. The fare, threepence, has gone up since Charon's time, but hardly in proportion to the cost of living. At the Museum I was told that the Roman exhibits had been removed to a new museum on the site of the fort itself. This is in Baring Street, which runs up from the hollow now occupied by Ocean Road to a hill known as the Lawe, overlooking the sea and the mouth of the Tyne. It was an obvious position for protecting the river mouth and the traffic which frequented it and here the Romans built a fort in the second century. When Severus launched his punitive expeditions into Caledonia this fort, covering five acres, sprang into activity as a great base. Elaborate storehouses were built, some thirty seals from which, labelled AVGG for Serverus and his sons, joint Emperors, and once attached to the stores here, are now in the Museum. These stores, and the troops, were dispatched from here by sea to Cramond on the Forth. At that time the garrison was the Fifth Cohort of Gauls, five hundred strong.

Early in the fourth century Constantius turned the store-houses, no longer required, and some of the granaries, into dwellings, each containing two rooms and a lavatory. This change has been connected with a change of garrison, for the *Notitia Dignitatum*, a list of the military and civil establishments of the Empire compiled in its final form about 433 but partly reflecting earlier conditions, shows the fort, which it calls Arbeia, as occupied by the Tigris lightermen (*Barcarii Tigrisienses*). Professor Richmond envisages them as employed to transfer cargoes from sea-going ships to flat-bottomed lighters for transport upstream, forerunners of the famous Tyne 'keels', but clearly they were some sort of light naval unit. Later still, after the Theodosian restoration, the fort became a fortified village occupied by farmer-troops and their families. Research has shown that it escaped the successive destructions which overcame the Wall and its forts, only falling when the barbarians put it to the flames about 400.

Behind the Museum about a quarter of the fort area, the central and western portion, has been preserved from modern building. Unfortunately the rain made it impossible for me to do justice to it. I was like a walking penthouse, with water pouring off my beret, my nose, my sleeves and the skirts of my raincoat. To our left as we approach from the Museum is a Hadrianic double granary, in which two tile-kilns were built in the fourth century. Behind these is a small Antonine granary and beyond that the headquarters building. Here we can see successive Hadrianic, Antonine and Severan work, the first two facing north-west, the last south-east. An exceptionally large strong room lay beneath the Severan shrine, with a barred window looking out on to the judgement hall. It needs little imagination to reconstruct the busy scenes which must have been enacted here when everyone was on his toes at the bidding of the masterful Severus. In the fourth century the administrative rooms each side of the shrine were provided with hypocausts for heating. Until then the clerks must have warmed themselves during northern winters on charcoal braziers. Behind one of these rooms is a stone wall, exceptionally well preserved.

To the south of all these buildings, occupying the other half of the exposed area, lie parallel Severan granaries, built over Antonine barrack blocks. At the end nearest the Museum is an Antonine water tank, once fed through settling tanks by water carried in bored tree-trunks from neighbouring springs.

It is never easy to clothe mere foundations in imagination with the massive structures which once surmounted them. A visit to the Museum will, however, help to repeople them with some of the living figures who once carried on their business hereabouts. Most moving of its exhibits is the tombstone set up by Barates, a native of Palmyra in the desert beyond Phoenicia, to Regina, a woman from Hertfordshire. Formerly his slave, she had become his wife, only to die at the age of thirty. Under the Latin inscription is written in Palmyrene script reading from right to left, 'Regina, freedwoman of Barates, Alas!' She sits in a basketwork armchair, her head surrounded by a nimbus indicating her departed soul, her wool in her work-basket beside her. What romance, what poignant tragedy, this one stone reveals! And by great good fortune we have her husband's tombstone at Corbridge, set up we know not by whom, when he too died at the age of sixty-eight. What, we inevitably ask, was this Asiatic (whose name, from Bar-Athé, means son of a semitic goddess) doing in north Britain, and how did he like it after the parching heat of Palmyra, that desert fortress which the Old Testament calls Tadmor in the wilderness and which Zenobia vainly defended against Aurelian? The inscription on his tombstone suggested that he was a *vexillarius*, which may mean either standard-bearer or maker of standards. Mr Birley thought he was too old for the former and that an Easterner would hardly become a soldier in Britain, whereas several such came here as merchants.

Another fine tombstone is that erected by Numerian, a trooper in the First Asturian cavalry, to his freedman Victor, represented reclining on a couch in the garden of paradise and served with celestial drink by a small attendant. There is also a remarkable sword lost about AD 200 outside the fort. X-ray examination revealed that its blade was pattern-welded from steel and iron twisted and hammered into a mass to produce a leaf-like design and that it was inlaid with golden bronze, with representations of

Mars in full armour on one side and an eagle between military standards on the other. After delicate cleaning, it is now exhibited in a transparent air-tight plastic container, a triumph, as the Museum justly claims, of ancient and modern craftsmanship.

Splashing valiantly through the rain, I snatched some tea and then returned to the Black Gate, where Mr Lewis had invited me to meet the honorary curator of coins, Mr J. H. Corbitt. I am afraid I made rather large drafts on his time, for I was glad to meet an expert in this difficult field. I knew of course that the imperial coinage was based, under Augustus, on the gold *aureus* and the silver *denarius*, twenty-five *denarii* going to the *aureus*, with the brass *sestertius* and *dupondius* and the copper *as*, worth respectively one-fourth, one-eighth, and one-sixteenth of the *denarius*. Also that the silver coins were gradually debased until under Severus their silver content had been almost halved, and that Caracalla replaced the *denarius* by the *antoninianus*, which was itself debased until in the fourth century the various silver-plated coins suffered the fate of the German mark after the First World War. But I had never made any serious study of Roman coins and it was a treat to be taken through them, with examples from the Society's fine collection. Mr Corbitt emphasized, what I had not fully grasped before, that the imperial government used coins as a means of publicity. One had had glimpses of this in the case of the usurper Carausius, who ruled Britain from 286/7 to 293. His coins advertised the equality of rule grudgingly conceded him by Diocletian and Maximian, and hailed him as Restorer of the Age and victor over the Germans. When we find the Emperors celebrating 'Concord' on their coins we can legitimately infer that there has been considerable discord, only recently patched up. Similarly, when late Emperors advertise the renovation of the Empire with *Salus reipublicae* and *Gloria romanorum*, we may be pretty certain that the Decline which led to the Fall has already gone far.

We also discussed the vexed question of the date of the final evacuation of the Wall, as evidenced by coin-finds. It has generally been assumed that the Wall was abandoned in 383, when Magnus Maximus crossed to Gaul. This seemed to be supported by the coin evidence, for the coins found on or near the Wall, with some exceptions, go down to 383 and then stop. This contrasts strikingly with the rest of Britain, where the coins go on to Honorius and Arcadius. But there have always been scholars who maintained that this evidence is inconclusive, as regards the Wall at least. There, it has been argued, we have far too few coins of the latest period to warrant any deduction from the absence of post-383 coins. Mr Corbitt showed me a recent article by Dr J. P. C. Kent of the British Museum, who claimed that he had re-examined many of the coins from Coventina's well and found five issued after 383 and up to perhaps 396. These had been sent to Mr Corbitt for his opinion and I was allowed to examine them. They looked like our old threepenny pieces and I could see very little on any of them, though apparently they had suffered in cleaning. I have since heard that Mr Corbitt inclines to support Dr Kent's theory and hopes to examine the whole of the Coventina hoard. His findings will be awaited with interest, for this hoard is so large that it should give us more representative data than is forthcoming from any other site. The whole question, with which is linked the larger issue of the date of the Roman evacuation of Britain, is of course bedevilled by the great falling off of the copper coinage on the death of Theodosius the Great in 395. Consequently the coin evidence must be used with care in trying to solve these problems.

I felt that I exhausted the patience of my kind hosts, so I left about nine, hoping fervently that the weather would be less wholesale on the morrow.

4

WALLSEND TO
HEDDON-ON-THE-WALL

Old men who have followed the Eagles since boyhood say that nothing in the Empire is more wonderful than first sight of the Wall.

KIPLING, *Puck of Pook's Hill*

Wednesday dawned grey but dry and my hopes rose as I at last set out on the first stage of my walk. Three considerations led me to start from the east – first that the indispensable Bruce-Richmond does so, secondly that the eastern end is the dullest and has fewest visible remains, so that I was anxious to be done with it, and thirdly that I have an unreasoning preference for travelling westwards, possibly an unconscious urge to move with the sun and to finish each day with it ahead of me.

So I took a train to Wallsend and walked riverwards down Station Road to Buddle Street. Here, at its junction with Hunter Street, stands Simpson's Hotel, built in 1912, and in its wall is a tablet recording that the east gate of the fort once stood a few yards away. The outline of the fort is marked by white stones in the cobbled roads, where it can be traced crossing Leslie Gardens and Davis Street and running along Winifred Gardens and Carville Road.

It will be remembered that the Wall was extended, on the narrow gauge, from Newcastle to Wallsend as an afterthought. No doubt it was soon realized that the high banks overlooking the bends of the Tyne prevented a proper watch being kept from the fort at Newcastle. So a four-acre fort was added at Wallsend, called Segedunum, which is said to mean 'strong fort'.

Its garrison was first the Second Cohort of Nervians, later the Fourth Cohort of Lingones, both from Gaul. The fort was surrounded by a ditch and furnished with four double gateways, the Wall joining it at the west gate. Excavations in 1929 showed that Wall and fort were built at the same time, but full investigation was not possible. Fort and Wall hereabouts were eagerly robbed from the earliest days – first for the Saxon priories at Jarrow and Tynemouth, then for medieval churches and castles, not to mention the quiet systematic removal by farmers down the ages. Then came the discovery of coal, when destruction redoubled in the scramble for wealth, and finally the erection of Victorian Wallsend and modern housing estates. All that now remains is a poor fragment of the north tower of the east gateway of the fort and a short section, six feet high, of the wall which ran down from the fort's south-east angle to the river, both now re-erected in Wallsend Park.

Standing in these drab streets, it is hard to realize that in Horsley's time the ramparts of the fort could be distinctly traced, 'though it had all been plowed and is now a very rich meadow'. This was still its condition in 1848, when Charles Richardson made the water colour now in the Laing Gallery showing the site as a grassy plateau with water in the east ditch of the fort. John Brand, in his History of Newcastle, said that John Buddle, senior (after whom, or his son, the modern street was named), had a house built in the south-west angle of the fort and that in 1783 two new wagon ways were made through the east part of the fort, which laid open the foundations and showed them running down to the river. 'Stones with inscriptions were found, but the incurious masons built them up again in the new works of the colliery.' Mrs Buddle told Lingard that in digging a cellar in their house they found a Roman well. John Buddle, junior, one of the most distinguished colliery 'viewers' or engineers in the North and manager of the Wallsend colliery, told Bruce that he had often noticed the Wall running down from the fort to the river when bathing in the Tyne as a boy. It was this end wall, a necessary precaution against intruders, that was revealed when in 1903 the slip for the *Mauretania* was prepared by Messrs Swan, Hunter and Wigham Richardson and the fragment secured for the Park.

I did not think much of Mr Buddle's road, or of Wallsend, though I must not be hard on a borough which is no doubt doing its best. Its inhabitants have at least the advantage over Londoners of being able to escape more easily from industrialism. But on that grey morning the prospect was not exactly attractive, especially when the rain again descended and accelerated into the inevitable downpour. Hastily donning raincoat and waterproof trousers and repeating Psalm 132, verse one, I proceeded to make the best of it, but it was like walking under a waterfall. I have seldom felt more ridiculous or engaged on such a pointless proceeding. After all, it was my idea, this mad walk, and now I was to reap the reward of my folly. 'Vous l'avez voulu, Georges Dandin', as the unfortunate peasant says in Molière's play. I might not have minded the rain, had it not frustrated all efforts to consult either map or guide. It is all very well to exclaim, with Hamlet, 'My tables; meet it is I set it down', but when the said tables are buried beneath waterproofs and the downpour turns all paper into a watery mass, settling down is out of the question. So, feeling more like a frogman than a walker, I stepped out on my first mile of the seventy-three, reflecting that whatever happened the weather could not get worse and could not spite me thus for ever.

Perhaps I was fortunate to have the rain, if rain there had to be, in this stretch. For there is little to look out for, and so I continued doggedly towards Newcastle. The course of the Wall is marked by a path lined with Roman stones in the enclosure of Carville Methodist Church, but after that one is left to the imagination. It ran on to Stott's House Farm and up to the top of Byker Hill. A water colour by H. B. Richardson in the Laing Gallery shows

Byker Hill in 1848 with its windmill and the wall ditch filled by a pond. Now a new housing estate is filling up the last vacant land. The first milecastle was at Stott's Pow, where Bruce reported the tenant as busily removing the stones, the second at Byker Hill, and the third where the Wall descended to the valley of the Ouseburn, now a desolate district which, when I passed through it, looked like the *descensus averno* of Virgil. These milecastles are equally spaced at much less than a Roman mile, thus supplying additional evidence that this section of the Wall was an afterthought.

I inquired at the shop by St Dominic's Church and was told of the excavations which traced the Wall at its southern end in 1928. Thence it ran from the junction of Gibson Street and Chatham Place to that of Grenville Terrace and Blagdon Street, and from there to All Saints Church, Silver Street. It then crossed the Lort Burn by the Low Bridge and so to the Castle at Newcastle. Alexander Gordon in the eighteenth century saw the Wall going 'straight to the Sally Port Gate' and Stukeley said that it joined the Castle 'where the stairs are', that is, the Dog Leap Stairs. Stukeley, in fact, saw a great deal. 'I pursued the Picts' Wall,' he wrote, 'beyond Pandon Gate going eastwards from Newcastle. It is very plain thither from Sandgate Mill, both the ridge of the wall and the ditch ... Having mounted the hill, a coal shaft is sunk in the very ditch, and here is a square fort [he means milecastle] left upon the wall ... Without the ditch is a coal-work lately set on fire, which vomits smoke continually, like a volcano: many more coalworks all about it.' Yet old Hutton found a green pasture here, 'with Severus' Ditch [he means the wall ditch] at the top, which is plain all the way to Newcastle'.

The fort at Newcastle is perhaps the greatest mystery of the Wall. Built in the heart of what presently became a busy town, its site was soon covered with buildings. Excavations in 1929 confirmed that it stood where the Castle now stands. Some walls and a hypocaust, with various

Roman objects, were then found, but its outline is still partly conjectural. It was clearly a small fort, perhaps only two acres in extent, which seems surprising for such an important position. For it was here that a road from the south crossed the Tyne by a bridge, called Pons Aelius in honour of Hadrian, this being also the name of the fort. Its building must have taxed the art of the Roman engineer. When the eighteenth-century bridge was demolished in 1872, Bruce watched the removal of one of the piers, where traces of Roman work were found. The Roman pier had been built by driving iron-shod oak piles into the river bed and fixing upon them a horizontal framework to carry the stone foundation. The pier had cut-waters at both ends and was thirty-four feet long from point to point. The bridge itself was apparently of timber; it has been estimated to have been over seven hundred feet in length and to have carried an eighteen-feet roadway. It remained in use, presumably with many repairs, until the fire of 1248, which destroyed most of the town. The altars to Neptune and Oceanus, mentioned above, are thought to have come from a shrine on this bridge. The *Notitia* gives the garrison as the First Cohort of Cornovians, from Shropshire, the only example of a British unit on the Wall, but there are suggestions of an earlier occupation by the First Cohort of Thracians.

After lunch in Newcastle, I resumed my westward way. To my surprise, the rain had stopped, and soon furtive patches of blue sky began to appear. The morning's gloom had vanished and the world was again full of colour. The Wall ran along the south side of what is now Westgate Road and breasted the long ascent of Westgate Hill. There is nothing of note in this not very elegant suburb, but near the top I passed a mission hall conducted by Pastor H. Harrison and displaying the text 'Ye shall not walk in darkness but in light.' Was this an omen? I have always rather despised the Romans for their childish belief in such things. Readers of Suetonius must often have been bored by them, but I reflected that I was now in Romania and might as well do as the Romans did. Nero, I felt certain, would have been immensely cheered by such a coincidence and such a message. So, feeling a foot taller, I strode on to the top of the hill, where at last I felt the good west wind full in my face and saw the green hills beyond Tyne gleaming in the struggling sunshine.

After resting in the bright new church of the Venerable Bede at Benwell, near the site of Milecastle 6, I made good speed to Benwell fort. Its site, just opposite the new Rutherford Grammar School, is curiously close to Pons Aelius, only just over two miles away. Placed advantageously on the top of the hill, with a steepish slope to its south, it occupied five and a half acres and was garrisoned first by cavalry, then by the first milliary Cohort of Vangiones from upper Germany and in the third and fourth centuries by the first *ala* of Asturians. Its name was Condercum, meaning the place with an outlook. The northern third of the fort projected beyond the Wall and is now under the reservoir north of the main road. The remainder is now covered by buildings, but Horsley found the fort distinct, though Hutton could only trace it by roughness in the ground. In his day Benwell was a village of ninety houses. The fort buildings were on the usual lines, except that the southernmost blocks were stables. In earlier days troopers were housed with their horses, but by Hadrian's time they were separated, each *contubernium* here measuring twenty-eight by eleven feet and housing eight troopers. An inscription found here bore further witness to the building of this fort under Platorius Nepos, in this case by units from the British fleet (*classis Britannica*).

The Vallum, which we now meet for the first time, deviated to pass round the south of the fort where, opposite the south gate, its steep-sided ditch was crossed by a natural causeway, the vertical sides of which were revetted in stone. This causeway was pierced by a drain to prevent the ditch being flooded. It carried a metalled road, on which was a massive gateway twelve feet wide with double gates. This feature has fortunately been preserved within railings in Denhill Park by the Ministry of Works, the only remaining example on the Wall. The Vallum ditch was later filled up around the fort to make room for the growing village. Of this the only visible relic is the foundation of the temple of Antenociticus, but this likewise has been saved and can be seen between the villas in Broomridge Avenue. Turn left down Weidner Avenue at the sign in the main road, then right along Westholme Avenue and left again into Broomridge Avenue.

This little temple is a gem in its neat simplicity. It was only eighteen by ten and a half feet with an apse for the god's statue four feet nine inches wide and six feet deep, smaller than the Christian church of Roman Silchester. One would give much to know what rites were celebrated here and what hopes and anxieties filled the hearts of the worshippers. All we know is that the god was youthful, if the head found here and now at Newcastle was his, and that the two altars now in the same museum flanked the apse, where casts of them still stand. One is dated under Marcus Aurelius and the other, erected by a centurion of the Twentieth Legion, is adorned on its sides by a vase for pouring libations and a knife for sacrificing animal victims.

Just outside the Vallum was a domestic or official mansion, eighty feet by sixty, with seven rooms and a furnace. Three hundred yards south-west of the fort were the baths, long since destroyed, but not before a plan of them had been made.

The sun was now shining so genially that I dispensed with my pullover and moved on in high spirits. The gloom of the morning seemed a thing of last year. At last I could echo that delightful medieval song –

> Levis exsurgit zephyrus,
> Et sol procedit tepidus;

though I must walk several more miles before I could complete it with

> Iam terra sinus aperit,
> Dulcore suo diffluit,

for I was not yet done with the miserable ribbon development which here unduly lengthens the escape into the
countryside. I must confess to a liking for these medieval
lyrics, which Miss Helen Waddell has made known by her
delightful translations, almost in preference to much of
classical Latin poetry, though without denying the great-
ness of the latter. No doubt this is poor taste, but Hadrian
himself had peculiar literary prejudices which made the
purists raise their eyebrows. One has to consider, not only
the excellence of the poetry, but its spirit. The classical
Roman poets, who had never known the miracle of the
northern spring or the hope which the Faith brought into
the world, lack something which these anonymous medieval versifiers have to perfection. Is there anything quite
equal to the poignant longing of

> Ut mei misereatur
> ut me recipiat
> et declinetur ad me,
> et ita desinat?

And when, one cannot help asking, is Miss Waddell to give
us another book like *The Wandering Scholars*, in which
supreme scholarship is distilled in haunting prose and the
music of fairyland? Such benefactors to the human race
should be compelled to produce a *chef d'œuvre* every five
years at least.

But to return to our Romans. From Benwell the Wall
continues for many miles along the south side of the main
road from Newcastle to Carlisle, which was built over its
ditch. The reason for this desecration is the Forty-five

Rebellion. When the Young Pretender reached Carlisle, General Wade was at Newcastle, but could not intercept the Scots for lack of a proper road to transport his artillery. Accordingly, after the failure of the invasion, orders were given to construct a military road (not to be confused with the Roman Military Way) between the two cities. Roger North, travelling from Newcastle to Hexham in 1676, wrote: 'We were showed the Picts' Wall, but it appeared only as a range or bank of stones all overgrown with grass.' Stukeley, writing of the making of the Military Road, said: 'The overseers and workmen employed by Act of Parliament, to make a new road ... demolish the Wall, and beat the stone in pieces ... Every carving, inscription, altar, milecastle, pillar, etc, undergoes the same vile havoc, from the hands of these wretches.' A few years later, in 1755, John Wesley came this way to preach at Nafferton, between Heddon and Corbridge. 'We rode,' he says in his *Journal*, 'chiefly on the new western road, which lies on the old Roman wall. Some part of this is still to be seen, as are the remains of most of the towers, which were built a mile distant from each other, quite from sea to sea. But where are the men of renown who built them and who once made all the land to tremble? Crumbled into dust.' Thus far only did that tireless evangelist speculate.

Our only consolation is that had the road not been made the Wall and its buildings would probably have suffered equally from farming operations; but one could wish that they had chosen the line of the Stanegate for their road. At some places it was possible in the last century to see the foundations of the Wall in the road in a dry summer, but tarmac has deprived us of even this.

Some distance beyond Benwell the road descends steeply to Denton Burn and then climbs as steeply beyond. Here the Wall must have presented a fine spectacle when, in all its original glory, it plunged into the valley and then majestically breasted the opposite slope. All this must now be recreated by the imagination. It was while descending this hill on another occasion with his stepdaughter and grand-children that John Wesley nearly lost his life. In the valley I had my first view of the Wall itself in its original position. Just before the Denton Burn, on the left of the road, on what used to be Thorntree Farm, a few yards of the broad Wall still stand, immune from further molestation, but flanked by a glaring hoarding. Why, one asks, must so much of what we have to see be spoiled by advertisements? Possibly the Romans would have offended equally had they had the resources of modern science at their command – posters advertising gladiatorial shows were found painted on walls of houses in Pompeii – but I am sure the Greeks would have condemned us as barbarians. True, we still illogically protect some things from this desecration – churches and castles, for example – but why, for instance, should our buses be plastered with feeble jokes and our stations uglified by those grotesque longshanks drinking rum? And why, in particular, are escalators dedicated to women's underwear? A problem for the archaeologist of the future.

Near the top of the hill, climbing from Denton Burn, Turret 7B and about sixty yards of Wall are preserved by the Ministry of Works. This is our first example of a turret, rising here to six courses on a flag foundation, and we can see how it is recessed into the Wall some five feet. It is thirteen by nearly fourteen feet internally. The turrets (which by the way are distinguished by the number of the nearest milecastle to the east, with the addition of an 'a' or a 'b' for the eastern and western members of the pair) are assumed to have had an upper storey, reached by a ladder resting on a stone platform in one of their corners, which can still be seen in many examples. Just beyond this I had my first sight of the Vallum, about one hundred and fifty yards south of the road. Farther on, the ditch of the Wall is clearly seen at many points just over the stone wall on the right of the road.

Pursuing my way through Walbottle, a dim little place, I

passed a branch road to Newburn, situated at the first ford over the Tyne. By this David II of Scotland passed to his defeat and capture at Neville's Cross in 1346, two months after the English victory at Crécy. The Romans had gone, but the Caledonians did not cease their incursions, though they received equal, if not more, provocation from the English. With the union of the kingdoms, Samuel Daniel could write

> No wall of Hadrian serves to separate
> Our mutual love, nor our obedience:
> Being subject all to one Imperial Prince,

but he was a trifle premature, for in 1640 the Scots under General Leslie cut up an English force at Newburn and then occupied Northumberland and Durham, thereby forcing Charles I to call the Long Parliament. The register at Newburn Church records the two marriages of George Stephenson. Here, too, was buried William Hedley, one of the pioneers of locomotive construction, whose 'Puffing Billy' built in 1813 and used at Wylam Colliery nearby, sixteen years before Stephenson's 'Rocket', is on view in the Science Museum at South Kensington.

After passing through Throckley, a straggling place, I at last emerged into real country. A little farther on I came to Great Hill, on descending which towards the village of Heddon-on-the-Wall a fine stretch of the Wall, about one hundred yards long, is seen preserved, six courses high on the south and four on the north at the maximum, on a flag foundation. Just before this, at the top of the hill, the Vallum is cut through the living rock and the marks of the Roman picks are plainly visible. I could not find this at first, but a little investigation led me to it. Go through a white gate on the left of the road with 'Please shut the gate' on it, up the hillock and through some rather troublesome gorse bushes and you will find yourself descending into the Vallum. It is worth turning aside to see.

I had intended to reach the next fort, Rudchester, that day, but it was now six-thirty and I had walked some twelve miles, besides doing some research in Newcastle Public Library. To go on would have meant walking back to Heddon, so I decided to call it a day. I did not trouble to make a possibly vain search for accommodation for the night, for I could easily start from Heddon on the morrow. So, *cansado pero contento*, I boarded a bus for Newcastle, bath and dinner.

Sestertius of Septimius Severus, commemorating his Britannic victory

5

HEDDON-ON-THE-WALL
TO PORTGATE

Ay, now am I in Arden, the more fool I; when I was at
home I was in a better place, but travellers must be content.
As You Like It, II, iv

Thursday the 17th June dawned fair and improved as the
day wore on. There was a bracing west wind, piling up
masses of light clouds, which rose swiftly and passed over,
missing the sun with marvellous dexterity. It was the finest
day of my walk as it turned out.

Saying goodbye to Newcastle, I was soon stepping off the
bus at Heddon and tramping along the Military Road,
which here carries straight on, while the main road forks
left to Corbridge and Hexham. I was now carrying my full
pack for the first time, since I must find new quarters for
the night and must therefore carry all my *lares et penates*
on my back. But I had cut these down to a minimum and
my ruck-sack nestled with surprising comfort into my back.
My walking shoes – I had treated myself to a pair of
Lawrie's hand-made marvels – carried me along almost in
spite of myself, like a walking pendulum.

In some respects this was my least interesting day, as
there are few remains of the Wall and its attendant structures to be seen in this sector. But the pleasant countryside
– a piece of typical unexciting rural England – and the
glorious weather, made it one of the most enjoyable. There
was little traffic and I was able to enjoy the profusion of
wild flowers and grasses which lined the road. The poor
weather of the preceding weeks had retarded even the

northern seasons and now the hedgerows and meadows were as attractive as any garden border and all the more so for being undesigned. Buttercups and cowparsley, of course, were everywhere, also deep red clover, plenty of crane's bill and the trefoil which carpets every odd corner with its yellow birds' feet tinged with red: but there were king-cups as well, shy pansies, ragged robin, wild mignonette, sorrel, translucent red in the bright sun, and, in larger clumps, dog roses and yellow broom brilliant after the rain. I almost wished I were a botanist, to know what it was I was seeing, though I have always thought that flowers are best left to the poets. The botanist is all too prone to give them a necessary but ugly Latin name and leave it at that. The anonymous medieval author mentioned above said in twelve words about all that need be said:

> Ver purpuratum exiit,
> ornatus suos induit:
> aspergit terram floribus,
> ligna silvarum frondibus.

For a mile and a half west of Heddon the Wall and Vallum run almost parallel and the ditches of both can be easily seen, that of the Wall just over the north wall of the road, the Vallum in the fields to the south. Just beyond the first cross-roads we reach Rudchester, the fourth fort on the Wall and nearly seven miles from Benwell. The *Notitia* calls it Vindobala and gives as its garrison the First Cohort of Frisians, from what is now Holland, but it was probably a cavalry fort at first. It covered four and a half acres, nearly one half of which projected north of the Wall and therefore north of the Military Road. Partial excavation has revealed six gates, of which four had double portals. Two of the gateways had had one of their portals blocked soon after erection, as their thresholds showed no sign of wear by wheels or even by boots. The others had probably been treated in the same manner. At one time this practice, found at many other forts, was ascribed to declining morale in the defenders of the late Roman period, but this evidence shows that it was the result of a change of policy, probably due to the building of Antonine's Wall. Even when the latter was abandoned the Wall zone was protected by outpost forts farther north, aided perhaps by irregulars operating as scouts beyond them, so that it was no longer thought necessary to provide for rapid sorties. The change may, however, have been inspired by the need to economize in sentries or guards. Part of the headquarters building, with its usual shrine and offices and underground strong room, was uncovered, and one storehouse. These strong rooms, by the way, were generally added to the forts in the early third century.

When Horsley came this way he found the ruins very considerable, but Lingard saw only an immense heap of stones and in 1820 the ramparts were down and the ditch scarcely visible. Modern excavations have left nothing exposed and all we can see is the outline of the ramparts in the grass, and a bath-like depression in the rock west of the farm, the purpose of which is unknown.

At Rudchester was found a life-size, but very coarse, figure of Hercules, now at the Museum at Newcastle. He now lacks head and feet, but still holds his club and an apple from the garden of the Hesperides and has a lion-skin over his left shoulder. Four altars were also taken from a temple erected here to Mithras. Similar temples existed at Carrawburgh and Housesteads. Mithraism is of peculiar interest, not only because it was popular with the Wall garrisons, but because it was perhaps the loftiest of the mystery religions and was for a time the most dangerous rival to Christianity. It sprang from the highly ethical religion of Zoroaster in ancient Persia, who saw the universe as the seat of a mighty contest between Ahuramazda, lord of light and goodness, and his satanic rival Ahriman. Mithras was the creation of Ahuramazda and after a miraculous birth slew a bull, from which came all the fruits of the material world, and was finally received into heaven. He thus typified the taming of wild nature and the ultimate salvation of the good. In its later form, Mithraism became a secret cult, whose members received a mystic revelation as they progressed through successive grades of knowledge, of which seven are mentioned by St Jerome. It had some sort of initiation by ordeal and a sacramental meal of bread and water, which Christians denounced as a travesty of their own Eucharist. Mithraic temples were built as long halls, flanked by divans for the worshippers and ending in a sanctuary containing a shrine with an image of Mithras slaying the bull, accompanied by two attendants, Cautes and Cautopates, with uplifted and lowered torches, typifying light and darkness respectively.

Mithraism was often associated with the cult of Cybele, in which initiates underwent the *taurobolium*, or blood bath, in a pit under a stage on which a bull was actually slain. Scholars differ as to whether this gruesome rite was adopted by devotees of Mithras: certainly no such pit has been found in the forts on the Wall. Mithraism made an instant appeal to the Roman soldiers, whose virtues it actively encouraged, but it seems never to have been a popular religion. For one thing, it was confined to men, and probably had its most earnest followers among officers and NCOs, though it was also favoured by clerks and slaves. Above all, it had no historic basis and thus disappeared, like its sister cults, before the rise of Christianity. One of the Rudchester altars, erected by a centurion of the Sixth Legion and now at Newcastle, shows Mithras grasping a bull by the horns in its lowest panel. Another records the restoration by a prefect of the temple of the Unconquered Sun, with whom Mithras was often associated.

The attentive reader may have noticed mention of several monuments put up by legionaries and perhaps have wondered what such were doing on the Wall, after they had completed its building. The answer is that detachments from the legions occasionally assisted the auxiliaries in holding the defences, while in some cases individual legionary centurions were seconded for duty there and might even command a cohort if an officer of knightly rank was not available. In the Museum at Carlisle is an altar to Jupiter from the fort at Maryport, set up by a centurion of the Tenth Legion, which never saw service in Britain, while in command of a Spanish cohort. Another such altar, now at Newcastle, was erected by a centurion of the Second Legion commanding the Lingonian cohort at Wallsend.

Later, on reaching Housesteads, I learnt from Dr D. J. Smith that the temple of Mithras at Rudchester had been located and excavated the previous summer by Messrs J. P. Gillam and I. MacIvor. Their report, recently published, shows that there were two successive Mithraea here. The first, built probably in the early third century, consisted of a nave forty-two and a half by twenty-six feet, with a stone bench on each side for the worshippers, a vestibule at one end and small apse, probably housing a relief of the god slaying his bull, at the other. The overall length of the whole building was sixty feet, exactly the same as that of the Mithraeum found in London in 1954. It was crudely constructed and no pains had been taken to secure correct alignment or symmetry. The vestibule had been carelessly built over a pit, into which it finally collapsed. Later, perhaps towards the end of the third century, the temple, without the vestibule, was rebuilt, in better work, on the old foundations. This second building was apparently abandoned after deliberate desecration some time early in the fourth century. We shall find two other temples of Mithras as we go along the Wall, at Carrowburgh and Housesteads. All seem to have flourished at the same period and to have come to a more or less simultaneous end, implying, the excavators here suggest, 'a single wave of feeling along the line of the Wall, or a single general order'. If this were so, one wonders whether it was due to the official recognition of Christianity at this time. On the one hand, that event must have greatly strengthened the struggling Romano-British Church: on the other, we know that other pagan cults continued to flourish in Britain for long after this. In any case, the Wall must have been one of the last districts to have felt the impact of Christianity.

Rudchester is splendidly sited on a platform of high ground, commanding magnificent views over the Tyne valley to the left and the hills beyond. The road descends somewhat and then climbs steadily to over five hundred feet at Harlow Hill, veering slightly to the right to do so, while the Vallum continues straight on till they are four hundred yards apart. The ditch of the Wall is very clear on this stretch. At the village on this hill I noticed the unusual surname Tulip on a garage, presumably of the same family as that Henry Tulip who aroused old Hutton's ire, as we shall see later. Here Hutton found the road charming, 'like a white ribbon upon a green ground'. Tar has dimmed this bright picture, to the comfort of the motorist. Aesthetes often complain of the disfigurement of the countryside by pylons, but these black ribbons are far more uglifying. We have grown used to them, but imagine how they would mar a Constable landscape.

Descending the hill, I came to the Whittledean reservoirs, lying placidly one on the right of the road and several to the left. Ascending again, I began to wonder whether I should obtain any lunch beyond the chocolate which was all my improvidence had provided me. But a little farther on, where the Vallum re-approaches the road, I spied what looked like an inn about a mile ahead. It was indeed the Robin Hood Inn, East Wallhouses, a neat hostelry whose car park is laid over the Wall ditch. Here I found some welcome sandwiches and cider. The proprietor has put out a brochure giving an excellent account of the Wall hereabouts, which he has obviously taken the trouble to get an expert to compile. But I rather doubted its statement that some authorities think that messages could be sent by heliograph from the Wall to Rome in about six hours. Was this technique then known, and, if so, would the British climate allow of its reliable use?

Opposite the Robin Hood the Vallum showed up well in a ploughed field. A little farther on, where a by-road turns off to the left by a grey stone cottage near the site of Milecastle 18, it is particularly distinct to the immediate east, with the causeways and the corresponding gaps in its mounds very clear. On the right of the main road at this point, in front of a pleasant farmhouse, the Wall ditch has been planted with rhododendrons and guelder-roses, which made a brave show as I passed. A mile or so farther on, at a cross-roads, I rested on the broad grassy verge almost covered with deep-red clover and variegated trefoil – a small matter to record, but a minor miracle at that moment. The afternoon, in fact, was as near perfection as I could wish, and after the recent gloom I was prepared to drink in the minutest beauties to the full.

After this the road climbs to Carr Hill, 682 feet high, but avoids the summit, which the Wall of course strides across. Here I sat on the edge of what was clearly a turret, presumably No 20A, opposite an attractive farmhouse. To the east I could see the Vallum approaching the farm until it ran under a wall, which crossed it like a switchback. One of the banks then emerged in the trim lawn in front of the house. I envied the owners of this delightful spot, as I drank in the marvellous view they had across the Tyne valley to the blue hills of southern Northumberland beyond, with scores of white clouds piling up against a vivid blue sky. Presently a tank roared by, frightening a very young foal which stood by its mother on the bank of the Vallum. I could gladly have lazed here for a couple of hours, but I still had much ground to cover and must move on.

Presently the Wall passes through a plantation on the left, while the Vallum descends the grassy hill in great vigour. Here it has the usual gaps in its mounds, but no causeways over its ditch, one of the places where the defacing was never completed. Signs of Roman quarrying are visible here. On regaining the road, I chatted with a motorist and his wife who had come out from Blaydon for the afternoon and spoke with enthusiasm of the countryside into which they could escape so easily from the grimy town. I have often thought that a lot of nonsense is talked these days about 'escapism'. One should accept one's lot if it cannot be changed, but if the cage is sometimes opened, it is surely better to escape for a time than to hug the bars, even though they be of gold. There is no need to develop a 'guilt conscience' about it. Even the Roman slaves had their fun and games when the Saturnalia came round once a year. The trouble with most people is that they don't know how to escape. They rush to seaside or country and then bury their faces in newstrash which they could have read as easily at home and which only takes them back in imagination where they ought to have stayed.

I was now nearing Halton fort, but failed to find the left-hand road marked on the map at that point. So I went on up the hill only to find that I had reached Portgate, where the Military Road is crossed by one from Corbridge to the north. This latter road was known in the Middle Ages as Dere Street, but was originally a Roman highway from the great base at Corbridge to the Forth. It was apparently built by Agricola and was later studded by the forts of Risingham, High Rochester, Cappuck and Newstead, the last on the Tweed. A few miles north of Portgate a branch called the Devil's Causeway ran off to the mouth of that river.

I had hoped, while at Corbridge, to find a bus which would take me to Risingham and High Rochester, but there was no such animal. High Rochester (Bremenium, meaning 'roaring stream'), over twenty miles up Dere Street, was built by Agricola as he advanced into Caledonia and was held until the great invasion of 367, after which Theodosius forbore to restore it. Its remains are still imposing and include a large platform for a *ballistarium*. Many of the stone projectiles for its use are preserved in the porch of the school-house at Risingham. This latter fort (Habitancum) was erected, some twelve miles north of the Wall, by Lollius Urbicus, when the frontier was advanced to the Antonine Wall, and was entirely rebuilt under Severus.

It was now well past tea-time, but I found only a closed inn, so must perforce do without. This matter of refreshment is one that they manage better abroad than we do. What earthly good do our legislators think they achieve by preventing travellers obtaining an innocent drink at any time? Do they really think that Englishmen would only make beasts of themselves without such restrictions? Or is there some special magic in the hours between three and six? It seems queer that the nation that invented 'five o'clock tea' should find such difficulty in obtaining it. Fortunately I can go all day if necessary without liquid refreshment, so I retraced my steps to the white gate I had missed. On the way down I had a splendid view of the Vallum vividly outlined in the golden sunlight as it descended Carr Hill.

The fort at Halton, seven and a half miles from Rudchester, originally contained four and a quarter acres and like Benwell and Rudchester was built with its front portion (*praetentura*) projecting beyond the Wall. It was garrisoned by cavalry – in the third and fourth centuries by the First *Ala* of Sabinian Pannonians, a detachment from what is now western Hungary, first raised by a certain Sabinus. The *Notitia* gives its name as Hunnum. It was built over the ditch of the Wall, for much deeper foundations were found where the ramparts crossed the line of the ditch, yet a slab recording the name of Platorius Nepos shows that the decision to add forts to the Wall was taken soon after the Wall was erected. Only the eastern half of the *praetentura* has been excavated, but three exceptional features were revealed. Besides barracks and stable blocks, a large hall, one hundred and sixty feet long, spanned the *via principalis* in front of the headquarters and is thought to have been used for parades or for exercise. A platform behind the north wall may have been designed to carry a *ballistarium* for discharging stone balls, one of which weighing a hundred-weight was found here. Roman artillery comprised three main weapons – the catapult, which fired arrows, the *ballista* or *ballistarium*, using stone balls, and the onager, which hurled larger stones by means of a sling. In each case power was produced by torsion from twisted gut; and a range of up to 500 yards may have been attained. The Wall and its forts were not designed to be fought from, but there is clear evidence of the use of *ballistae* at the outpost forts of High Rochester and Risingham and therefore nothing impossible in their use here. Smaller structures at House-steads, once similarly interpreted, are not now so regarded. There is a model of a catapult in the museum at Corbridge.

The other special feature in the *praetentura* was an elaborate bath house, the only example on the Wall of internal baths for the garrison, as distinct from the com-mandant's private suite. Apart from these peculiar features in the *praetentura*, Halton is unique in having been en-larged, at a later date, by enclosing a further half-acre on its west side, giving it a queer L-shape. The reason for this extension, and why it was confined to this fort, can only be guessed: possibly it was found necessary to increase the garrison in order to protect the neighbouring Dere Street.

As at Rudchester, the excavations were not left exposed. But one can easily make out the ramparts and internal buildings as mounds in the grass, as well as the southern ditch. I longed to know what was underneath. Plunging my penknife into the mounds about fifty times, I encountered stone as often as not. My hands itched to grasp a spade and start digging there and then. It seems strange that so little excavation has been done here. South of the fort similar traces of the *vicus* can be seen.

When Horsley was here he was shown part of an aque-duct, just within the east wall south of the main road, by a countryman, who told him that 'it was what the speaking trumpet was lodged in'. This was a commonly-accepted tradition. Camden says: 'The dwellers hereabouts talk much of a brazen trunk (whereof they found pieces now and then) that, set and fitted in the wall artificially, ran between every fortress and tower, so as that if any one on what tower soever conveyed the watchword into it, the sound would have been carried straightways without any stay to the next, then to the third . . .' There was, of course, no such system of speaking tubes and this fable was no doubt derived from a misunderstanding of the numerous aqueducts and water-pipes. We are, in fact, rather in the dark as to the method by which signals were sent along the Wall. Polybius describes a method of sending messages by light-signals, and Vegetius says that fire, smoke and sema-phore were in use. The reliefs on Trajan's Column show what are generally regarded as signal towers, of wood two storeys high, with what looks like a stick, probably a torch, projecting from their upper windows and also beacons ready for lighting. No doubt the Romans would not have built so many turrets on the Wall, not to mention signal towers elsewhere, as on the Yorkshire coast, unless they had a reliable system of sending messages from them with convenient speed. This is one of the subjects on which we would gladly have, and may some day secure, more light.

I had now to find my way to Corbridge for the night. It was a very pleasant walk downhill on a perfect late after-noon – and how few such there were that year – but it somehow seemed a very long three miles. The path from the fort led me past a charming miniature castle and a miniature church, just the sort of castle I could really covet, with a squat square tower at one end and two slender taper-ing brick chimneys like miniature Wren steeples. This Hal-ton Castle was the seat of the Carnaby family in the late Middle Ages and was burned by the Scots in 1385, after which the present tower was built. The following century the house was extended to the north and in the seventeenth the east wing was added with its unusual chimneys. Both castle and church, the latter rebuilt in 1706, contain many

Roman stones. In the churchyard is an inverted Roman altar which used to stand in a nearby lane, when it was the custom to carry coffins, going to the church for burial, three times round it, no one knows why.

The Carnaby family sprang into prominence under Sir Reynold Carnaby, who exploited his service to Henry Percy, the unstable sixth Earl of Northumberland in Henry VIII's time, to obtain valuable grants of land, including a lease of Corbridge. Then he curried favour with Thomas Cromwell, obtained Hexham Priory on its dissolution, and became keeper of Tynedale. But he was despised as an upstart and, when the North rose in the Pilgrimage of Grace, Halton was unsuccessfully besieged by Sir Thomas Percy, the disgruntled brother of the childless Earl, and by John Heron. Thomas was executed at Tyburn, but Heron got Carnaby's keepership. Sir Reynold died in 1543, a few years after being captured by Tynedale rievers, and his line came to an end in 1699.

At Corbridge, after some search, I found a comfortable room at the 'Golden Lion'. After a bath and a good dinner – for it was a long time since I had breakfasted in Newcastle – it was pleasant to watch the sunset from the ancient bridge, built in 1674, while the river murmured peacefully below. To one brought up to associate the Tyne with coaly Newcastle, it is always a revelation to discover that for most of its length it can vie with the choicest streams of Wales or of Scotland. *Fies nobilium tu quoque fontium.*

6

PORTGATE TO CHESTERS

Ainsi de peu à peu crut l'empire romain,
Tant qu'il fut depouillé par la barbare main,
Qui ne laissa de lui que ces marques antiques,
Que chacun va pillant ...

JOACHIM DU BELLAY

Friday was again fine, but colder, with a blustering wind piling up great clouds, through which the sun somehow managed to shine most of the time. My first concern was to call on Mr William Bulmer, honorary curator of the Museum at Roman Corbridge, whose models at Newcastle we have already noticed and who kindly spared time to answer my numerous inquiries about the many subjects in which he is an expert. I arranged to devote the afternoon to Corbridge and to complete a further stage of the Wall while the weather held during the forenoon.

Walking rapidly back to Portgate, I was soon following the course of the Wall westwards once more. Here I was on a high plateau, rising to eight hundred and sixty feet at its maximum, the highest so far. The views were exhilarating, extending quite twenty miles on both flanks and ranging from the hills to the south-west which I had enjoyed earlier to the Cheviots far away to the north, of which I now had my first sight. Most thrilling of all, far ahead I could see the wild country where I hoped to be next week, with the Wall faintly but unmistakably climbing peak after peak. On my right the Wall ditch was in fine condition, the north bank being very steep and clear cut: at one spot the original upcast can still be seen just beyond it. Here the Vallum was at its best so far, its causeways being very plain. Old

Hutton was so entranced by the sight that he burst into rhapsodies which sound strange in such a prosaic character. 'I climbed over the stone wall,' he wrote, 'forgot I was upon a wild common, a stranger, and the evening approaching ... lost in astonishment, I was not able to move at all.'

I followed his example, but did not express my enthusiasm so feelingly. I found the distant prospects equally attractive. For we have now left cultivated country for the most part and are entering those great wastes of moorland which, if less pretty, have a charm all their own. In fine weather one has a greater sense of space, and at all times the comforting feeling that, whatever happens, one is free from the tentacles of the town. Here are no streams of traffic, no overcrowded pavements, no stifling tubes filled with humans condemned to an ordeal from which other animals are protected by law. How strange that each new purgatory invented by science should be hailed as another milestone on the march of Progress! 'Wonderful London!' the asinine papers shout, as their proprietors glide from flat to club in large cars, while their strap-hanging readers can hardly open their pages for the crush. Meanwhile I was free for the time being: free to stand erect, to stride along without hindrance and to see horizons all round me – this last one of the greatest and least appreciated joys of existence.

Somewhere just beyond the highest point in this sector the wholly broad Wall is replaced by narrow Wall on a broad base, to continue thus to the Irthing. Just before the modern milestone marking eighteen miles from Newcastle the outlines of Milecastle 24 (Wall Fell) are quite plain. After another mile or so, where the ditch is again very deep, the road begins its long descent to the North Tyne. At the hamlet of Hill Head a centurial stone recording the century of Caecilius Clemens of the Eighth Cohort is to be seen built into a farmhouse, but this I failed to find, being misdirected by a van-driver. A little south of this was a Roman

quarry where a quarryman had written 'The stone of
Flavius Carantinus' (*Petra Flavi(i) Carantini*) on the rock.
There were wall scribblers then as now, but as their work
always invites imitators the stone has been removed to
Chesters Museum.

Here the road turns south for a space, leaving the Wall to
run between it and St Oswald's Church on the hill to the
right. At the side of the road is a wooden cross with a tablet
inscribed:

> HEAVENFIELD
> WHERE KING OSWALD BEING ABOUT
> TO ENGAGE IN BATTLE ERECTED
> THE SIGN OF THE HOLY CROSS AND
> ON HIS KNEES PRAYED TO GOD AND
> OBTAINED THE VICTORY AS HIS
> FAITH DESERVED. A.D. 635
> LAUS DEO

The date should be 633. Oswald's adversary was Cadwallon, king of the Welsh, who in the previous year had
combined with Penda, the heathen king of Mercia, to defeat
and slay Edwin, the first Christian king of Northumbria.
But Oswald, of the rival Northumbrian line, who had been
converted while an exile in Scotland, rallied the northern
English and advanced to defeat the Welsh invader. Bede
tells the story and adds: 'The place in the English tongue is
called Heavenfield ... near the wall with which the
Romans formerly enclosed the island from sea to sea ...
Hither also the brothers of the church of Hagulstad (Hexham) ... repair yearly on the day before that on which
King Oswald was afterwards slain, to watch there for the
health of his soul and, having sung many psalms, to offer
for him in the morning the sacrifice of the holy oblation ...
for it appears that there was no sign of the Christian faith,
no church, no altar erected throughout all the nation of the
Bernicians, before that new commander of the army ... set

up the cross as he was going to give battle to his barbarous enemy.' The actual site of the elevation of the cross appears to have been north of the church, where lies Hallington, formerly Halidene (holy valley), but Cadwallon was slain in the battle the following morning at Denise Burn (now Rowley Burn) some seven miles south.

Descending the hill, I found a fine piece of the Wall near Planetrees Farm, preserved by the Ministry of Works. It is about thirty yards in length, rising to six courses on a flag foundation: on its south the original broad foundation and remains of a drain can be seen. We owe this fragment to the entreaties of Hutton. 'Had I been some months sooner,' he wrote, 'I should have been favoured with a noble treat ... a piece of ... wall seven feet and a half high and two hundred and twenty-four yards long: a sight not to be found in the whole line. But the proprietor, Henry Tulip, Esq, is now taking it down, to erect a farmhouse with the materials.' When Miss Mothersole came this way in 1920 she found thorn trees growing along the top of this stretch of Wall and threatening to disintegrate it, but the Ministry has averted this danger. Planetrees Farmhouse lies in the ditch of the Vallum, which continues below it and to its west.

Farther down the hill Brunton House is seen on the left. I obtained permission to go through the grounds, by way of a wood, to the field below, which can also be reached by a path from the road after it bends left at the bottom of the hill. Here another fine stretch of Wall is preserved, with the ditch covered by trees which fringe the field. In it is Turret 26B, the first turret known and one of the best preserved. It stands over eight feet high on the north side and four on the south. It is the first turret built with a section of the broad wall on each side, though on the west this continues to the end of the section preserved here and not, as the books say, for a few yards only.

We are now in the valley of the North Tyne, one of the loveliest parts of the county, with the river running clearly over its smooth stones and delightful woodlands nestling below the hills on each side. Here the Wall for the first time for any considerable distance parts company with the road and it was a pleasant change to follow its course, though no stones are now visible, through the fields to the river. The Tyne must have presented a not inconsiderable obstacle to the wall-builders, who met the challenge by a massive bridge. Its eastern abutment can still be seen and should on no account be missed. A fenced path leads to it from the south end of the modern bridge at Chollerford.

The eastern abutment of this bridge will be found high and dry some yards to the east of the river, which has since shifted its course considerably to the west. The Wall approaches its old bed to end in a tower twenty-two feet square. The abutment is built around this, its western face in line with the tower and of the same width, from which it recedes diagonally on each side. It was built of massive stones, securely bound together by iron rods set in lead, and still standing in places six feet high. The lewis (or louis) holes by which the separate stones were lifted into position can still be seen. This name is said to come from Louis XIV, whose engineers used this device. A small slot was cut in the stone, broader within than on the surface: two iron wedges, each expanding on one side to fit the slot, were then inserted, leaving a space between them for the later insertion of a third wedge with straight sides, the three completely filling the slot and being provided with holes at their tops through which the lifting tackle was then inserted. The system is sound but must have used up many man-hours of arduous labour.

Three stone piers supported the bridge: they have cut-waters on their northern ends only, which was a mistake, as it encouraged the eating away of the foundations on the south. One pier is under the present east bank of the river, the others can be seen in its bed when the water is low. The western abutment, partly destroyed by the river's change of course, still awaits excavation, but was apparently similar to its eastern counterpart. The bridge itself was of wood,

capable of carrying a road twenty feet wide, for several of
the scattered stones bear grooves into which its timbers
must have fitted, although Camden says that the bridge
here was arched. He also remarked that the country folk
hereabouts were of a warlike nature and slept out-of-doors
in huts with their flocks from April to August.

Close inspection of the eastern abutment will reveal a
lozenge-shaped mass of stones embedded in the larger
body. This is a pier of an earlier and narrower bridge,
carrying only the Wall or its walk. Part of another pier of
this earlier bridge can be seen in the second later pier. The
earlier bridge has been shown to be Hadrianic: the date of
the later one has not been ascertained, but in the interval
the river had already shifted considerably to the west. The
later bridge was less neatly built than the earlier one, a
change attributed to faulty supervision. But no doubt the
later builders managed to find something to criticize in the
earlier one, *more suo*. The Roman worker was probably
just as inclined to say 'Who's been spoiling this 'ere?' as his
modern British counterpart.

Running under the abutment and the tower is a channel
designed as a mill-race for an undershot water-mill, an
invention brought to Britain by the Romans. One of the
stones lying on the abutment is thought to be an axle-tree
from this mill, being fitted with slots for spokes.

Immediately beyond the Tyne we come to the fort of
Chesters, situated in the grounds of the eighteenth-century
mansion. It is reached by the road running west from
Chollerford, the entrance being indicated by a sign-post.
This being private property, a small fee must be paid,
but the pilgrim will not begrudge this for his first sight
of a fort whose chief remains are still visible above ground.
He will also thus obtain admission to the Museum on the
site, founded in memory of that ardent antiquarian and
former owner of the estate, John Clayton, and housing his
magnificent collection. Lovers of the Wall are indebted to
Clayton more than to any other man. Not only did he make

the first scientific excavations of forts and milecastles, and create a new interest in the archaeology of the Wall, he bought up whatever portions came into the market and thus saved them from probable destruction. In the end he owned five forts on the Wall.

Chesters, called Cilurnum in the *Notitia*, was one of the larger forts, covering five and three-quarter acres. Five and a half miles from Halton, it was admirably placed to guard the river-crossing on high ground immediately to its west. It had a cavalry garrison – in the third and fourth centuries the second *ala* of Asturians, though there are suggestions of an earlier occupation by the Augustan *ala* of Gauls. One wonders how these Spaniards liked the Northumbrian climate. True, the Asturian mountains have their share of inclement weather and there are places in Spain which are proverbially credited with *nueve meses invierno, tres meses infierno*. Nine months of winter they might often find here, but three months, or even one, of burning hell, never. No doubt they often drew the equivalent of their 'British warms' tightly around their shivering limbs.

The fort has the usual plan and like the three last we have visited had its *praetentura* extending north of the Wall. Like Halton, its *via principalis* had been built over the wall ditch. Recently, too, the foundations of the broad Wall and of a turret were found beneath it.

One reaches the fort by its north gate (*porta praetoria*). This had double portals, each about twelve feet wide and arched back and front. Each portal had double doors swinging on pivot-holes which can still be seen and closing against a central stop-block rising out of a sill. This arrangement may seem to sacrifice convenience for traffic to security, but two-horsed vehicles would find no difficulty in making the passage. Though these foundations do not require us to reconstruct the fort buildings entirely by imagination, as at our previous forts, we must remember that they are only foundations. Our imagination must still be called on to clothe these stones with their original superstructures. On each side of the gate was a guard-chamber surmounted by a tower, perhaps twice the height of the walls of the fort, which would be the same height as the main Wall. These towers were entered by narrow gateways from the portals and were pierced by the parapet walk along the top of the fort walls, so that sentries could pace the entire length of the defences without obstacle. As at Rudchester, the west portal of this gateway had been blocked soon after erection. The blocking was removed by Clayton to show the original work, but the sill is still unworn, while the eastern portal has had its sill and stopblock renewed at a later date. One can also see remains of a covered aqueduct feeding the fort at this point.

It is not easy for the novice to follow the arrangement of the fort, as its walls have not been preserved in their entirety and the fragments of buildings which survive have been fenced in, forming detached groups. But if, with the help of the guide obtainable at the lodge, we keep the plan in mind, it should not be difficult to understand what we are looking at: indeed, this little piece of detective work should add to the interest of our visit. The outlines of the ramparts can be seen as grassy mounds. Following these, we can easily find the main eastern and western gateways (*portae principales dextra* and *sinistra* respectively) and the south gate (*porta decumana*). All are similar to the north gate. The east gate is especially well preserved, rising to twelve courses in one place. Both portals of both east and west gates have been blocked soon after erection, their inner entrances as well, in the end, the spaces between being filled with rubble. The south gate was blocked in its west portal only, like its northern brother, but its east portal continued in use and was several times destroyed and rebuilt on the fallen débris – mute witnesses to the inroads of the Caledonians in 197, 296 and 367. We shall not miss the Wall coming up to the south tower of the west gate, some six courses high, and we may notice that the guard-chamber of the north tower of this gate has been

made into a settling tank late in its history, fed by another
aqueduct. We can also see an interval tower east of the
south gate, and the south-east angle tower, twelve courses
high. These angle towers were set diagonally at the rounded
corners of the fort. Between this angle tower and the main
east gate is a single-portal gate: there was a fellow to it on
the west wall, making six gates in all, as at the previous
three forts. Where a fort was supplied with six, instead of
four, gates, the subsidiary gates were set at the end of the
via quintana.

The headquarters building, railed off in the centre of the
fort, was on the usual plan. The underground strong room
under the 'chapel' was apparently built under Severus,
whose coins were found on its floor. There was a local
tradition that the fort contained underground stables from
which ghostly horsemen used sometimes to emerge and
silently roam the countryside of nights. When the strong
room was uncovered, the workmen believed that this was
the entrance to the stable. The curious thing is that the
strength of the ghostly army corresponded with that of the
Roman garrison so many centuries ago. Is this an example
of folk memory, or had the story been constructed from
some overheard remarks of an antiquary?

East of the *principia* was the commandant's house, supplied with baths, from which a statue of Neptune was recovered. The rest of the fort area was filled with the usual
barracks, stables and granaries.

Turning towards the river, we come, just below the
western abutment of the bridge, to the troops' bath house.
This is well preserved and will repay careful study with the
aid of a plan. These Roman baths, whether for private or
military use, followed a general plan, though some were
more elaborate than others. The intending bather first
entered a dressing-room (*apodyterium*), where he stripped:
at Chesters this room stands at the northern end of the
block and was forty-six feet long and thirty wide, supported
by pillars. When excavated its floor was completely paved

with large flags. On its west end were seven round-headed niches, unique in Britain: their object is uncertain, some thinking them meant for holding the bathers' clothes, others for unguents and other appliances used in the baths. To its east was a latrine, with a drain running down to the river. Then the bather passed through a vestibule into a long room extending southwards: this was the warm room (*tepidarium*), heated gently by a hypocaust. Beyond this was the hot room (*caldarium*), where the sweating bather was scraped down with a strigil, made of horn or metal: on its right was a hot bath (*alveus*) and at its end a boiler room (*vasarium*) to supply this. The *alveus* is apse-shaped in a square bay, whose walls stand impressively high. Parallel to this block was another containing a second and later warm room, and on its north a small room thought to be an *unctorium*, where the bather was well rubbed with oil. Returning to the warm room, he could complete the course by turning east from the vestibule into the cold room (*frigidarium*), where the bottom of a basin can still be seen, with drain leading to the main drain. If he was fearful that his pores were not really closed after his earlier warming-up, he could pass into the cold bath to the east. He might, however, have first turned west from the vestibule into the sweating room (*sudatorium*), with its own furnace, for this room, unlike the warm and hot rooms already entered, which were heated by hot air under the floors or in the walls, was fed by hot air direct from the furnace, which burnt charcoal to prevent fumes and smoke. Elsewhere timber was used for fuel, though coal is known to have been used at several of the forts, as it was at the temple of Sulis at Bath.

The invention of the hypocaust system of heating is generally ascribed to C. Sergius Orata, a contemporary of Cicero. The hot air from the furnace (*praefurnium*) was conducted through an underground channel to a pillared vault beneath the room to be warmed: this was paved with tiles on which numerous other tiles (at Chesters tufa blocks)

were placed to form small pillars, supporting the floor of
the room above them. Where great heat was required flues
made by hollow tiles were inserted in the walls and similarly supplied with hot air. That the system worked can be
seen from a story related by the younger Pliny in his letters
of an oppressive master whose slaves attacked him and
threw him on the heated floor to see whether he were still
alive, an ordeal which he survived for the time being by
feigning death.

It can be seen that the troops had opportunities for
recreation on bath-days. Judging by the numerous inscriptions set up to the goddess Fortune in military bath-houses
we may guess that the dressing-rooms were the scenes of
much riotous gambling. An altar to this fickle deity, crudely
carved with her figure holding what looks like a trident but
is probably a cornucopia, and set up by a German called
Venenus, was found in this bath-house and can be seen in
the museum.

One cannot avoid the impression that these bathing
establishments became something of a fetish with the
Romans, like the traditional Englishman eating his Christ-
mas pudding in the tropical wilds in evening clothes. Yet
they must have made the ordinary Roman far cleaner and
pleasanter than even monarchs of later centuries. It is dis-
tressing to reflect that after Roman days most people,
medieval monks, proud nobles, even Shakespeare and Dr
Johnson, might have offended our modern noses.

These baths also indicate, by their consistent plan, the
strong sway of custom, even among that practical people.
We must remember that only with recent industrialization
did habits and fashions begin to change rapidly. Before the
first civilizations arose, major changes in these respects
represent the passing of centuries, and the same slow tempo
was to resume its course during the Dark and far into the
Middle Ages. It was largely a matter of incentive. Where
competition was keen, as in warfare, men would strive to
outdo rivals or enemies: so weapons develop or are re-

placed by new inventions, while other spheres of life are more static.

South-west of the fort traces of a large village have recently been discovered by aerial photography, which revealed a main road with several wide streets leading off it, all lined with buildings. The cemetery was farther off, by the river.

There is so much to study in the Museum that only a few samples can be mentioned here. Most attractive are several fine sculptures – one of Cybele, the Great Mother, standing on a bull (indicating her domination over all creation), from the south-west corner of this fort, a recumbent river-god, thought to represent the Tyne, also found here, and a fine figure of Victory holding a palm branch, from Housesteads. A relief of a standard-bearer, with sword, shield and standard, though much worn, gives a vivid impression of the appearance of the Wall's defenders. Then there is an altar to Minerva from Carrawburgh set up by one Quintus, who calls himself *architectus*, apparently a soldier with qualifications in that line. Building operations here are illustrated by a tablet recording repairs to the Tyne bridge and another the provision of an aqueduct by the Asturians under the governor Ulpius Marcellus late in the second century. This general was a stern and, if a later writer can be believed, a rather cranky martinet. He is said to have had his biscuits sent him from Rome, to ensure that they would be stale, in spite of his toothless gums. This strikes me as a silly story, for he could easily have arranged for local products to be left till stale. It is also related that he used to write out before retiring a series of orders to be sent to his lieutenants at intervals during the night, thus keeping them on their toes and making them think he was watching over everything when actually sound asleep.

There are also some lanky Roman milestones from the neighbourhood, for both the Military Way and the Stanegate were supplied with these, many centurial stones, and others commemorating the Twentieth Legion by its emblem, a wild boar. There is a fine bronze measure from Carvoran, a slab which has been used as a draught-board, some sling-stones, many interesting tools, weapons, combs and other personal belongings, which help to reconstruct the life of the people hereabouts. Many other exhibits relate to forts further on and will be mentioned in their place.

Perhaps the most interesting discovery at Chesters was a diploma issued to an auxiliary trooper on completion of his twenty-five years' service, one of only six found in Britain. This came from the south gate and is now in the British Museum, but a replica is to be seen in the Museum here. It consists of two thin bronze plates hinged so as to form a four-paged booklet. It is a long-winded document, mentioning all the eligible units then serving in Britain, but it would be precious to its owner, since it not only granted him full citizenship but legalized his marriage with any wife. Roman law recognized various forms of marriage and the troops did not wait for official blessing on discharge to acquire informal partners. The diploma is dated 146, under Antoninus Pius, whose titles it recites with all the prolixity of officialdom.

I felt that I was now due for a rest and made for the 'George' at Chollerford for a snack lunch. Then I returned by bus to Corbridge and walked out to the 'dig' at Corstopitum. But Corbridge deserves a chapter to itself.

7

CORBRIDGE

If you would take the pains but to examine the wars of
Pompey the Great, you shall find, I warrant you, that there
is no tiddle taddle nor pibble pabble in Pompey's camp: I
warrant you, you shall find the ceremonies of the wars, and
the cares of it, and the forms of it, and the sobriety of it,
and the modesty of it, to be otherwise.

Henry V, IV, i

Corbridge is a lovely town, full of sedate grey stone houses
unspoilt by jarring modern colours, the recent villas being
placed unobtrusively on its outskirts. Perched high above
the broad Tyne, which it spans by a bridge built in 1674, it
has all the charm of a Cotswold market town without the
accompanying noise arising from the turning of the Cots-
wolds into one large aerodrome. Its broad main street,
almost without shops, is graced by the ancient Angel Inn
and pleasant houses overlooking the river, their gardens full
of eager-bright flowers after the recent rain. From here
three narrow roads converge on another square where
stands the church of St Andrew. Behind, the fields climb to
the ridge along which runs the Wall, while southwards
across the river wooded hills rise gradually. Altogether a
pleasant place, in pleasant weather.

The town was burnt by Robert Bruce in 1312, but it had
already been the scene of a Danish victory over Scots and
English under King Constantine in 914. At the east end of
the main street is Low Hall, a late seventeenth-century
house, the nucleus of which is a medieval pele tower three
storeys high with stone stairs in the thickness of its walls.
In the churchyard is the Vicar's Pele, a fortified vicarage
of about 1300. The town sent two members to Edward I's

Model Parliament, but was never again represented. By the church I noticed with an involuntary thrill a sign-post pointing the way to Otterburn. I should have been scarcely more surprised had it said Camelot or Lyonesse, for Chevy Chase, fought there between Hotspur and Douglas in 1388, belongs rather to legend and ballad than to sober history with a local habitation.

Corstopitum, the Roman station at Corbridge, lies half a mile west of the town on a plateau overlooking the river to the south and the Cor Burn to the west. King John came here in 1201, having heard that treasure was hidden in the remains, but when his men found only stones marked with bronze, iron and lead he left in disgust. When Leland came this way he found the town 'full meanly builded', but 'among the ruins of the old town is a place called Colecester, where hath been a fortress or castle. The people there say that there dwelled in it one Yoton [Old English for "monster"] whom they fable to have been a giant'. In 1644, during the Civil War, the Scots, who under Leslie were investing Newcastle, sent a detachment to secure the ford across the Tyne here. This was attacked outside Corbridge by Royalist cavalry from Hexham, who routed the Scots in a spirited charge. But Newcastle fell, after the parliamentary victory at Marston Moor.

It is advisable to visit the museum on the site first, to get an idea of what we shall see on the ground, though the chief treasures are indicated by notices. Unfortunately the new guide, by Mr Eric Birley, was still in the press, but it has since appeared. Corbridge was the easternmost fort, so far as known, on the Stanegate, constructed by Agricola from Carlisle eastwards and defended by other forts at Nether Denton, Chesterholm and Newburgh. The first fort at Corbridge was built by Agricola about AD 79. It was surrounded by a double ditch and turf ramparts, and contained wooden buildings: its area was about nine acres. It was a cavalry fort, built to guard the bridge over the Tyne, some stones of which can be found with difficulty when the water is low. The garrison was almost certainly the *ala Petriana*, a Gaulish unit one thousand strong, and the only cavalry regiment of its size in Roman Britain at any time (there were only a dozen such in the whole Empire). This bridge was over a hundred and fifty yards long and, as finally built, about twenty feet wide. For it was here that the easternmost of the great north roads of Roman Britain came up from York, via Catterick and Binchester, to cross the Tyne, and, as Dere Street, to lead to the Forth.

Agricola's fort was burnt at some time after AD 100, perhaps in connexion with the disaster that overwhelmed the Ninth Legion. It was then replaced by another of four acres, partly overlapping it, and the *ala Petriana* was transferred to Stanwix, outside Carlisle.

When the Wall was built, the value of Corbridge declined. For a time it was unoccupied, though still maintained; but the Roman reoccupation of Southern Caledonia under Antoninus Pius gave it new life. For Scottish campaigns a great base to the rear was essential and so in 139 Lollius Urbicus, the builder of the Antonine Wall, established a new depot at Corstopitum, roughly on the site of the second Flavian fort, and on the plan of a normal wall fort, facing south. It was of half-timber on stone walls and was supplied with barracks, granaries and a hospital. Its headquarters was recently discovered towards the southwest corner of the Severan storehouse mentioned below. The work was done by detachments from the Second Legion, easily spared now that Wales was quiet. There was much rebuilding, of poor quality, in 163, when S. Calpurnius Agricola was sent over to deal with a mysterious revolt: the hospital and some of the barracks were taken down. The presence of detachments from the other two legions is shown by inscriptions. Particularly interesting is the large tablet recording work done by the Twentieth Legion: this was assembled from several fragments, two rescued from the Pele at Low Hall, and the complete text restored by the ingenuity of Mr W. Bulmer, honorary keeper of the museum. The depot was destroyed, like the Wall, by the incursion of 197, coins of Pertinax (193) being found immediately under signs of burning.

The subsequent history of Corstopitum is best followed in the open air. When L. Alfenus Senecio restored the Wall and his master Severus once more led the legions into Caledonia, Corstopitum was thoroughly rebuilt as a military base. It shared with South Shields the work of supplying the arduous northern campaigns, though curiously enough no traces of the presence of Severan armies have been found on any of the roads into Scotland. If we turn right on leaving the museum we come to the end of the main road (the Stanegate) dividing the depot from east to west. To the north of this road are Severus' reconstructed granaries, their massive floors still standing on their ventilation pillars. Built over their Antonine predecessors, they have external buttresses to take the weight of their stone-slate roofs and in front of each granary are four pillars which held roofs over loading platforms. Next is a fountain, supplied by an aqueduct from the north, which ran over the site of the earlier hospital. Then comes a large square building (Site XI) covering over an acre, with large rooms opening on to a central courtyard. This is generally called a storehouse, but Mr Birley suggests that it may possibly have been intended as the headquarters of a new legionary fortress. But it was never completed, owing to the abandonment of Severus' Scottish campaign by his sons on his death at York in 211. Its south-west wing was roofed later, but elsewhere the walls rise only a few courses and on the north only the foundations were built. But its massive rusticated stone blocks are witnesses to the grandiose schemes of that emperor. Along the side of the road are the bases of what must have been handsome columns, making porticoes which must have added dignity to the main thoroughfare. A reconstruction of this drawn by the late Paul Brown can be seen in the museum. Though made in 1938 it gives a reasonably accurate idea of the settlement's appearance at the height of its activity. Note how the buildings are bright with colour inside and out. This was true of the interiors of medieval churches likewise. Only with the Puritans did England assume drab monotones.

On the south of the main road lie two large Severan compounds, each with an ornamental gateway opening on to a road running southwards, a short distance down which was the site of the south gate of the Flavian fort. The west compound contained workshops in which arrow-heads were made and other iron work was carried on by armourers from the Second Legion. The east compound contained officers' houses and the living quarters of another unit. Its north–south walls have a switchback appearance through subsidence due to their being built over the ditches or walls of earlier structures. Each compound had its own headquarters building and water supply: relations between the two units seem to have been sometimes strained, for a tablet commemorates the restoration of concord between the Sixth and Twentieth Legions. The western headquarters had an elaborate 'chapel', containing a dedication to the Discipline of the Emperors and a relief of Hercules slaying the hydra, inspired by Athena: under it was the usual strong room, the steps down to which are exposed.

Fronting the road at the farther ends of the compounds were groups of temples. Each stood on an elevated *podium* after the usual classical style. Temples and compounds are separated by irregular walls, indicating that the former were built first and were outside the military area and also sacred, their cults being private but tolerated. We are not able to say what god was honoured in each temple, but Corstopitum provides more evidence on the cults of the legions than any other site in Britain. Besides those mentioned, altars and dedications have been found to Jupiter, Mars, Juno, Minerva, Victory and Rome among official cults; while unofficial deities include Jupiter Dolichenus, the Great Mother (Cybele), Hercules of Tyre, Astarte and Apollo-Maponus (the only British cult found here). In the

first of these Jupiter is equated with a god from the holy hill
of Doliche in Asia Minor and is grouped on an altar erected
by a centurion with the goddess of the Brigantes and with
Salus (Good Health). The inscriptions to Hercules of Tyre
and Astarte, the Ashtoreth of the Old Testament, form a
pair, as their cults were associated, and are unusual in
being in Greek. That to Hercules mentions the name of his
chief priestess, Diodora. There is also an inscription to the
Unconquered Sun, set up by the Sixth Legion under Calpurnius Agricola. The god's name was later erased, perhaps
because it referred to the hated Commodus, who saw himself as *Sol Invictus*, as he certainly tried to usurp somewhat
of the worship of Hercules; and, fittingly enough, several
water gods and nymphs were honoured here. Englishmen
have been derided for having two hundred religions but
only one sauce, yet the Romans could vie with them in the
former respect.

Most curious of all is the Celtic god Taranis known
locally to the irreverent as 'Harry Lauder'. His image was
found in Temple VI on a mould for reproduction on
pottery. He carries a Roman shield and helmet and a Celtic
wheel, symbol of the sun, lies at his side, indicating his two-
fold origin. This Taranis, mentioned in Lucan's *Pharsalia*,
was a major deity of the Gauls, and was appeased by
human sacrifice. But his roguish face, his knobbly knees,
and his twisted stick are pathetic revelations of the groping
of these far-off people for spiritual satisfaction. What feelings, what aspirations, we wonder, filled the hearts of the
poor folk who put their trust in this grotesque being?

The streets of the depot were lined with shops and
taverns. Outside a flourishing civil community grew up,
especially after Severus allowed the troops to live out of
camp. This was one of the few 'towns', like Aldborough
and Carlisle, in the north of Roman Britain. It has not all
been excavated yet, but is known to have extended for a
considerable distance outside the depot on all sides, except
perhaps the south. At any rate, several houses or shops

The Emperor Hadrian. *Bust in the Museo Nazionale, Naples*

Top: Down Hill and the Vallum in 1848. *From a painting by H. B. Richardson in the Laing Art Gallery, Newcastle.*
Bottom: The bath house at Chesters – the dressing room

Top: The hypocausts at Chesters, showing the system of conveying heat in channels under the floors of the rooms. *Bottom:* Brunton Turret

DM · REGINA · LIBERTA · ET · CONIVGE
BARATES · PALMYRENVS · NATIONE
CATVALLAVNA · AN · XXX

Monument to Regina, wife of Barates. *South Shields Museum*

Stone stele dedicated to Coventina, found at Carrawburgh.
Chesters Museum

IMPERATORIBVS CAESARIBVS
M AVRELIO ANTONINO AVG TRIBVNICIA
POTESTATIS XVII COS III ET L AVR
ELIO VERO AVG ARMENIACO TRIB
VNICIAE POTESTATIS III COS
VEXILLATIO LEG XX VV FEC SVB CVR
SEXTI CALPVRNI AGRICOLAE
LEGATI AVGVSTORVM PR

Top: Inscription recording work done by a detachment of the XX Legion under Calpurnius Agricola, AD 163, as restored by W. Bulmer, Esq, Hon Keeper, Corbridge Museum. The darker parts are original.
Bottom: The strong room at Corbridge, west compound

Top: Corbridge Colonnade in front of the granaries from the north-west. *Bottom:* Mithraeum at Carrawburgh immediately after excavation

Figure of the god Taranis ('Harry Lauder'). *Corbridge Museum*

have been found on both sides of the Stanegate just west of the granaries. In one of these was found a bronze jug containing one hundred and sixty early imperial gold coins. There were also many buildings north and east of the great storehouse, in one of which was a furnace where a piece of iron over three feet long was found. Signs of pottery manufacture and of smelting have been discovered, and two tombstones show that Latin was understood. The extent of this settlement was recently revealed by aerial photography: streets flanked by buildings branched off on both sides of the Stanegate and to the west a large Romano-Celtic temple was disclosed. Presumably this settlement had some sort of corporate life, with limited self-government, like the humbler *vici* outside the Wall forts. We must remember that Corstopitum covered some forty acres, of which only four have as yet been properly explored.

When Corstopitum was again overrun in 296 by the barbarians, they destroyed the temples, whose ruins were levelled and built upon by Constantius Chlorus when he recovered Britain for Diocletian. He also united the two compounds and converted the officers' quarters to industrial use. We cannot tell whether the failure to restore the temples was due to Christian influence. Constantius was more tolerant than his superiors, but Christianity had not made much progress in Britain at this time.

After this the depot sank in importance, but the civil settlement continued to flourish. Overlooking the river was a large corridor-type house (*mansio*), rather like that at Benwell, and thought to have been a station for the imperial post. It was one hundred and fifty feet long by seventy broad and faced south, with a terrace in front of it: it had an elaborate bath-suite. Here was found the 'Corbridge Lion', a realistic sculpture of a lion standing over his victim, part of a fountain. From the fourth century, apparently, dates the Corbridge 'Lanx', a beautiful solid silver rectangular dish, now owned by the Duke of Northumberland, of which a replica can be seen at Newcastle. On it is a

fine relief depicting Apollo and Artemis with their mother
Leto, and Athena and attendant animals. Such a treasure,
thought to have been made in the East about the time of
Julian, and a hoard of coins covering the years 364–85,
suggest that civilization and some luxury still prevailed.
But the end was near.

Corstopitum was again destroyed in the great barbarian
invasion of 367 and again restored, this time by Count
Theodosius, who may have built a rampart round the
whole settlement. This is the last known event in its history.
It almost certainly survived the supposed abandonment of
the Wall in or just after 383, for coins down to about 395
have been found here. It must be remembered that the issue
of coins declined greatly after 395 and that the topmost
layers of the site were pretty thoroughly robbed in the succeeding centuries. Much, no doubt, will be ascertained from
future excavation, but at present it looks as if Corstopitum,
like many other Romano-British sites, just faded away.
Two generations later small groups of English invaders had
found their way here, as their burials show.

It is the great disadvantage of Romano-British history
that, though we can reconstruct much of its social life, we
can people this with so few living individuals. To the
Empire's historians Britain was a mere outpost, only merit-
ing mention when recording frontier wars. To poets she
provided a little local colour, as when Horace aspires with
the Muses' help to visit the *Britannos hospitibus feros*. How
much more we should know, if only Britain had produced
an Ausonius, sketching in his memoirs and poems the aris-
tocratic society of his province and chatting in his letters of
his innocent small doings, his literary excursions and his
rhetorical triumphs. Such a one might have filled Corstopitum with flesh and blood, have given us the table-talk of its
messes and the gossip of its busy streets, sung the beauties
of its Tyne as 'the hill-tops waver in the rippling water',
told of the loves, the joys and the tragedies of its private
lives. All this we must try to do for ourselves, and we are

not quite without food for our historical imagination. The appearance of the place can be got from Paul Brown's picture, that of the legionaries from Mr Bulmer's statuettes, photographs of which are in the museum, of a centurion and of a private fully accoutred for kit inspection. Let us, then, attempt a stroll through the depot some fine May day in the early third century, while the Emperor Severus is campaigning in Caledonia.

Corstopitum is well behind the battle zone, but discipline is unrelaxed and sentries pace the defences of the military area. Within, corn from the granaries is being loaded into wagons for dispatch up Dere Street to the imperial base in Caledonia. An orderly is taking a note of the loads, writing with an iron *stilus* on a wooden tablet smeared with wax. Further on, a mixed crowd is seen round the fountain – a fatigue party drawing water to clean out the barracks, women from 'down town' waiting to fill their pots, a bit gipsy-like perhaps, but some, we notice, sport bright combs in their hair or sparkling brooches on their mantles. Opposite, we hear the clang of metal and, peering through the unglazed windows of a workshop in the west compound, we catch sight of brawny arms hammering vigorously as they turn out the swords, spears and arrows for which the troops are always clamouring in their gruelling campaigns up north.

Behind, in the headquarters building, a detachment is drawing its pay, brought up by guards from the strong room below the 'chapel'. One man is grumbling at the compulsory deduction for the army savings bank, others examine with curiosity the image and superscription on the new coins. Some appear impressed by their proclamation that all's right with the world, but a veteran, remembering similar pronouncements by the feckless Commodus, seems sceptical. Presently they break off and make westwards for the taverns and shops which line the Stanegate. There are not many shops, for the 'town' is after all only a large village. They are long, narrow buildings, windowless and opening straight on to the street, but their counters contain a surprising variety of goods. Fresh fish from the river, oysters and other shell fish from the North Sea, for the Romans were great lovers of these, carcasses of meat and other eatables, cloth materials of various sorts are displayed. We are perhaps surprised to see the butcher using chopper and steelyard which look almost modern. Do we see our friend Barates from South Shields, resigned by now to the loss of his Regina? At any rate, there is an obvious oriental trying to sell a choice length of cloth to the wife of an officer of the Sixth Legion, who has just alighted from her litter borne by slaves. She wears a red mantle, drawn over her head, and under this a blue tunic descending to her feet, and carries a purse, like a small shopping-basket, by a handle from her wrist. Her other hand holds that of her small son – Julian, is it, or Julius? for we cannot quite make out his quaint Latin baby-talk – *dimidiata verba* – as he prattles to his mother, and shoots a childish joke at the slaves, suggesting that their lot is not too hard.

Then there are trinkets of many kinds – pipe-clay figurines of naked Venuses and of Mercury from Gaul, and domestic utensils in metal and pottery. Some of the metalwork is attractive, as are a few glass vessels from the Rhineland, but the pots are *très ordinaire*, for the best days of 'Samian' ware are over and the stuff now in vogue is rather poor. But the villagers are pleased with the massproduced articles and gloat over the uncouth figures of naked goddesses and gladiators with which they are decorated. More attractive are a few vases and beakers, ornamented with lively animals or white barbotine scrolls, just arrived from Castor in the Midlands, but most of the pottery is rough but serviceable local work. Prominent are the lamps, looking like miniature feeding-cups and giving only a scant light from their oily wicks, but prized as the best thing obtainable.

We shall not enter the taverns, for the noise is deafening and there is hardly any room. But we can glimpse the potbellied *amphorae* from which the innkeeper fills the mugs of the drinkers. Some of these are singing snatches of ribald songs, while others throw the dice or quarrel drunkenly. *Meum est propositum in taberna mori* is the burden of their song, though the words are different, for many centuries are to run before that verse is coined. There are no licensing hours to 'kepe yow fro the whyte and fro the rede' and 'they' are open all day. Nor are there any football pools, but the rude image of Fortune on the wall reminds us that gambling is the natural outlet for unemployed minds and hands in all ages.

As we go along the main street we see more wagons into which stores are being loaded from the great building on its north, but we note that most of this structure is still in course of erection and that gangs of men are busy bringing up huge stone blocks and hoisting them into position. We hope that the lewis holes are well made and that none of the stones will drop on some unlucky worker. Farther on, we pass a party of uncouth men leading a troop of fierce dogs. These are the famous British hunting dogs, prized throughout the Empire for their strength and tenacity and shortly to be put aboard ship at South Shields for export. Turning down the side street to the south, we try to pry into the officers' quarters in the east compound, but are moved on by determined sentries. We manage, however, to learn from passers-by that in the *principia* beyond the commandant is administering discipline to a small group and that yesterday he conferred several distinctions, including the *corona aurea* on a centurion for bravery in the field and a silver standard on a meritorious unit. We will not follow the small party which presently moves off to flog two defaulters, for though the 'Discipline of the Emperors' looks fine on a handsome inscription it is not so pretty in practice, necessary as it may be in these martial days, when that stern Moorish master of the world is only a few miles away. It is not so long ago, we hear, since a man was sent down to York to be crucified for a particularly brutal murder. We are glad to notice, as we hurry on, that many of the troops, at any rate, are enjoying themselves in their guild house farther down the street. Had we come earlier, we are told, we should have witnessed the colourful ceremony of honouring the standards; but tomorrow we can enjoy a cavalry display, when squadrons of riders from Hunnum Fort, arrayed in scarlet tunics and yellow-plumed helmets covering their faces, will show their skill in complicated evolutions and sham fights with wooden swords.

Our spirits are now raised by a bright procession making its way towards one of the temples. A robed woman, who appears to be a chief priestess, for she has female attendants, moves slowly as if in mystic trance, while devotees follow intoning some mysterious chant. The crowd watches with intense curiosity, discussing in low tones the relative merits of this oriental cult compared with their own particular fancies. We overhear a superior-looking person telling his friends that these partisan worships are now outmoded and that up-to-date philosophers see a unity underlying this diversity. It is time, he says, to scrap the lot, or at least to leave them to the superstitious multitude: the intelligentsia should worship the One behind them all. His friend asks what he thinks of this new Christian sect, which seems to have the same aim, though he has not run across any of them in Britain yet, but our philosopher only shrugs his shoulders. Another oriental superstition like the rest, he seems to say.

From the depot we go out to the civil settlement. In contrast to the stately buildings of the former, this seems a huddle of small stone houses with thatched or tiled roofs, interspersed with many flimsy huts. There seems to be no order at all, but on entering we find that we can make our way along irregular muddy streets with narrow lanes turning off at intervals. Smoke rises from holes in the roofs and there are few windows. But we find a few shops, where native craftsmen display their humble wares, and not a few taverns. The people seem cheerful enough and children, dogs and hens frisk happily in the streets. Looking into an open doorway, we see a woman weaving on an upright frame; elsewhere we see others spinning, deftly twisting the lengthening line of yarn, with spindle and whorl at its end, as it unwinds from the distaff. Others again are busy grinding corn, their muscular arms turning the heavy querns, from which the meal slowly emerges. Peering into the lowly houses and cabins, we may catch sight of a housewife preparing 'herbs and other country messes' for the pot which hangs over the open wood fire, pounding the food in a round *mortarium* with gritty bottom.

We may wonder where the men-folk are, until we look up and see groups of them busy in the distant fields, some ploughing with two-ox teams, others cutting and hauling wood for fuel. And here is the village smith, grimy before the forge in his humble cabin, making a merry clang as he mends a ploughshare, while his boy plies the bellows and a peasant woman waits to have a knife sharpened, the only one she owns. But not all are busy. A few topers can be heard singing raucously in a tavern and outside two youths are half-quarrelling as they urge their suit to a local belle, who watches with non-committal superiority the outcome of their rivalry. And here are the inevitable gossips, hard at it, though there are no fences to talk over. In many matters the world wags much as it has always done, and will do: it is only the outward forms that change. Most of the folk speak Celtic, in contrast to the Latin which pervades the depot, though even there the orientals speak Greek or some eastern tongue when conversing between themselves. But even in the village some of the 'locals' contrive a Latin of sorts when it comes to dealing with visitors from the depot.

We are now on the edge of the cliff looking down to the Cor Burn. Modesty forbids that we enter the public baths here, but the sounds which rise from them tell us plainly what is going on. A ball-player counts his throws in strident tones; another cries shrilly as the hair-plucker plies his task. We can hear the masseur's palms going slap-slap on a fat torso, and, in between, the puffing of some would-be strong man as he swings heavy weights back and forth. *Res est arduissima*, but no doubt others are just enjoying a good 'waller' in the hot bath and are less vocal.

Continuing our way, we pass the cemetery which, as always in Roman times, lay outside the 'built-up area'. Here we can exercise our minds by trying to reconstruct the life-stories of officers and men from many parts, whose ages and length of service are recorded on their tombstones. More interesting, perhaps, are the rather pathetic memorials to small children, whose figures are crudely cut (or are they unconsciously striving towards the sublime puerility of so much modern art?). One youngster of five seems to be dressed in nothing but a smock: while another called Ertula holds her ball in her hands. Her age is given as exactly four years, sixty days, and though this sort of thing is quite common, sometimes indicating a belief in astrology, it surely argues considerable affection and therefore sadness when this small person was taken from her parents. We see another slab set up by a father 'to his dearest daughter Julia Materna, aged six'.

As we leave, we meet a strange sight – a detachment of soldiers, headed by a centurion, escorting a group of wild-looking men bound in irons. Caledonian prisoners, they must be. Few prisoners are taken in Severus' punitive expeditions, or if taken, few survive: but some have been spared – for slavery. In a few weeks they will be working in the fields outside some southern villa, or allotted to masters in Londinium or Corinium. It is a depressing spectacle, but life is hard in these days. But presently we are cheered by the sight of a detachment of legionaries returning from the front for a well-earned rest. All are a bit worse for wear: some are limping and a few stragglers are being helped on by their comrades, perhaps first-aid men told off for this task. But all are in high spirits and they march rhythmically to the beat of a resounding song. It sounds like *Ecce Caesar nunc triumphat qui subegit barbaros*, but perhaps we are mistaken. We seem to remember that the legions of the great Julius sang something of the sort in Gaul; and that was a long time ago.

Stepping out of our time-machine (which has perhaps rather muddled the different periods, but its controls are not too steady), we return to the present. The visitor to Corstopitum should not miss Hexham, only three miles away. Not only has it a magnificent priory church, with a Saxon crypt, built by St Wilfrid about 675, but these were largely constructed of Roman stones from Corstopitum itself. Built into the crypt is a slab dedicated to Severus and his two sons, with the name of Geta, the younger, defaced after his murder by his jealous brother. We need not shed many tears over him, for both were pretty low scoundrels. Such defacements were common in the third century, when palace revolutions followed one another as quickly as in some Latin-American republics today. In the nave, destroyed by the Scots in 1296 (when they also burnt to death two hundred boys in the Grammar School) and not restored till 1907, are many Roman relics, and in the south transept is a large memorial to Flavinus, a standard-bearer of the *Ala Petriana*, shown riding down a Briton, who tries to hamstring his horse. This stone certainly came from Corstopitum and since it must be earlier than AD 98, when an addition was made to the title of this unit for services under Agricola, it commemorates the earliest days of the fort.

St Wilfrid was a masterful, but not very lovable character, a forerunner of the imperious prelates of the Middle Ages, more concerned to advance the interests of their local churches than with the inculcation of true religion. His career foreshadowed that of Becket, whom I have always thought over-praised. An early visit to Rome made him the tireless champion of the papacy against the still independent Celtic church which, cut off by the English invasions, had fallen out of step with the rest of western Christendom. At the Synod of Whitby in 664 his appeal to the text 'Thou art Peter' clinched the adhesion of Northumbria to the

Roman obedience. This was undoubtedly a 'good thing', for it meant that England was brought within the main stream of western civilization and her church governed by sound administrators, instead of running to seed in the excesses of Celtic monachism. But it was just this sound statesmanship which Wilfrid resisted, when he opposed the division of his huge diocese of York by Archbishop Theodore of Canterbury, appointed by the pope himself. Yet the pope supported Wilfrid – hardly the best way to make the new system work. Wilfrid was banished and employed his leisure in converting the heathen kingdom of Sussex. A new king recalled him to a truncated diocese, but he quarrelled with his monks and then with the king himself. Again the pope supported him and eventually he returned as Bishop of Hexham. Those were rude times, but there must have been something wrong with a bishop who was so often in hot water. Nevertheless, he was a notable builder of churches in the North, scarcely yet Christianized, and his influence for good may have atoned for his obvious faults.

Hexham was a cathedral city for a century and a half, until it was merged in 821 with the see of Lindisfarne. The church was burnt by the Danes in 875 and refounded as a priory of Austin Canons in 1113, most of the present building dating from around 1200. In the market place nearby Henry Beaufort, Duke of Somerset, was beheaded in 1464 after his defeat by Lord Montague a few miles away. This was the last fling of the Lancastrians against Edward IV. The site of the battle appears to have been on Swallowtrees Hill near Linnels Bridge, two miles south-east of the town. Poor Henry VI escaped, but the picturesque incident of his Queen's rescue by a robber did not take place after this battle, as she was then in France trying to enlist support.

The visitor will not fail to explore the medieval and later treasures of Hexham Priory, remembering, if he is not altogether unthinking, that this was built to the glory of God and that its upkeep costs money. But we must return to our Wall.

8

CHESTERS TO HOUSESTEADS

Hills peep o'er hills, and Alps on Alps arise.
POPE, *Essay on Criticism*, 232

Saturday the 19th June was again fine. Rain was promised, but failed to arrive, though the clouds rose threateningly, and later a few gleams of sun struggled through them. There was a strong wind all day, straight in my face, bracing though impeding me, but at least it kept the rain off.

I was soon at Chollerford once more, following the Wall's course along the Military Road past Chesters, where it emerges from that estate. In a short time the road began to climb Walwick Hill. The last lap is pretty steep, but at the top the view was again exhilarating, with the noble pile of Hexham and the silvery Tyne in the valley to the left and range upon range of hills beyond. Here the road runs for a time on the berm of the Vallum, whose ditch is just off it to the left, while the Wall ditch stands out grandly about eighty yards to the north. This is all fine country, the road still rising gradually, with occasional minor falls. After passing some plantations I came out on to a grand open stretch and there, on the right, on Black Carts Farm, was the longest stretch of the Wall I had seen so far. It appeared to be between three and four hundred yards long, with a slight gap, and rose to a height of six feet.

In this sector of Wall is Turret 29A, now enclosed in a fence and encumbered with nettles. It is recessed as usual into the Wall, which is again of the broad gauge for a space on each side of the turret: its north side rises to fourteen courses. Somehow this stretch of Wall gave me a greater thrill than the trim sections so carefully preserved by the Ministry of Works, which have an atmosphere as of a public park. Nevertheless, it would be better if all the remains were under the Ministry's care. This section, for instance, is overgrown with trees and bushes, which cannot fail to damage it in time. Negotiating the shrubs and nettles, I managed to seat myself on the wall of the turret and eat my modest lunch of apple and chocolate. As usual, I had not troubled about lunch or tea, knowing that I should get a good dinner at Corbridge. I had considered and rejected the carrying of a vacuum flask as adding to the weight of my pack with little compensation. One can overdo being prepared for every eventuality. It is better, I think, to be comfortable and to risk a little hunger and thirst. The sun had at last penetrated the clouds and I could almost bask in its warmth and enjoy the rest and the clear solitude. Not a creature was in sight and the road to the south was deserted. Indeed, I had hardly seen more than half a dozen cars all that morning.

Resuming my walk, I soon reached the highest point of the plateau here, Limestone Corner, where the road bends from slightly north to slightly south of west. This is the northernmost point on the Wall. It is also one of the grandest sections of the whole walk. One really feels on the roof of the world – a hackneyed phrase, but truly applicable here. We are only 823 feet above sea, but the precise height does not matter. What matters is that one is above all the surrounding country. Then, and only then, one achieves that exhilarating certainty that all earth and all heaven are at one's command, that one has made this particular piece of country one's own. And far away were the blue outlines of Cross Fell to the left and the Cheviots to the right, magnifying the sense of space by providing the remotest possible framework to the whole view.

At the summit is Milecastle 30. To the left the Vallum is in fine shape, here cut through the solid rock and now filled with spring flowers. The Wall ditch, on the right, is even more exciting, for, just past the summit, it is unfinished and one can still see the huge masses of stone half cut from the rock and then left by the Roman engineers. In some, holes cut to lift them can still be seen: but for some reason the task was never completed.

After this the Wall rejoins the road and the ditch is just to the right. We now enter a long stretch which descends very slightly to Carrawburgh. For some reason I found this sector slightly depressing. The view is still extensive, but there is a feeling of desolation, such as moorland so often gives, when even the brightest day seems to presage dirty weather. Perhaps the geology or herbage is different here, perhaps the absence of trees was accountable, or maybe it was only my fancy. In Roman days even these uplands would be clothed with oak, birch and alder, while the valleys of the rivers and burns would be filled with thick forest. And so, passing Carrawburgh Farm and Milecastle 31, its outline very clear on the left, I came to Carrawburgh fort. For the help of southerners, it may be mentioned that the last syllable of this name is pronounced 'bruff'.

This fort, only three and a half miles from Chesters, is called Procolitia in the *Notitia*, meaning the place infested with badgers. It covers three and a half acres and was garrisoned first by the First Cohort of Aquitanians, then by that of the Cugernians (Belgic Gauls) and finally, in the third and fourth centuries, by the First Cohort of Batavians. These last must have found its breezy uplands a contrast to the riverside flats of their homeland. At first sight Carrawburgh disappoints, for little of the actual fort has yet been excavated: but it has several interesting features. The outline of the ramparts can be seen in the field: it will be noticed that the *praetentura* does not extend beyond the Wall, as at the last four forts we have visited. Carrawburgh was, in fact, a slightly later fort than most, perhaps ten years later, as is shown by the proximity of Milecastle 31 and, more certainly, by the fact that the Vallum does not deviate to the south to avoid it. Instead, it runs straight on, parallel to the Wall, and the fort was built over it. Apparently it was found that the gap of nearly eight miles between Chesters and Housesteads left a weak spot in the defences. The problem is involved with others to the west and awaits further investigation and sorting out.

One cannot help wondering why this fort has not been excavated. There has, it is true, been much excavation outside it. On the slope to its west were the unit's baths, similar to those at Chesters, but smaller. Among the floor slabs of its hypocaust were found two tombstones, now at Chesters, put to this base use long after the memory of the defunct had been lost. One had been erected to Aelia Commendus, wife of Nobilianus, an officer commanding a contingent of cavalry attached to the infantry cohort. The other commemorated a standard-bearer, shown fully equipped and holding a small shield in his left hand. His right grasps his standard, displaying the figure of a bull at the top and having three prongs at its base for planting in the ground. One wonders from what part of the Empire this Aelia came and how she passed her time in this remote outpost as the wife of a not very high officer. Perhaps she pined for her sunny homeland, but more probably she was a local woman, married while Nobilianus was still in the ranks. Had she companions in like case, with whom she could gossip and play the Roman equivalent of bridge? Did she visit other forts or seek relaxation in the modest amenities of Corstopitum? These are some of the questions I should like to have answered, for I can get no light on them from the books, but no doubt I am asking the impossible. All these people must have had their private lives, but we have no key to unlock their secrets.

The high light at Carrawburgh is the Mithraeum, excavated as recently as 1950. It will easily be found in the hollow south-west of the fort, the only piece of exposed stone-work on the site. It looks a bit naked, just four stone walls nine courses high, with a door at one end, like a barn

sunk in the earth. But we must once more use our historical
imagination. Originally the walls stood free: it is the
ground which has risen around them by deposit of peat.
There were three successive Mithraea here. The first was a
simple second-century building only twenty-six feet by
eighteen externally, containing a gravelled nave seventeen
and a half feet long and fifteen wide, with a stone bench on
each side, a small vestibule at one end and a smaller sanctuary at the other. Early in the third century the sanctuary
was extended a farther fourteen feet and at its end was
added an apse six feet deep. Later the interior was completely refitted and floored with flags and cobbles, upon
which heather was laid, and later still the floor was
boarded. Many chicken bones were found, relics it would
seem of ritual sacrifices, and in the sanctuary a brazier or
laver. The vestibule disclosed traces of a hearth and a
shovel was found here for feeding a charcoal fire with pine
cones brought from the Mediterranean. Most interesting of
all was an ordeal pit in the vestibule, just large enough to
hold a man lying full length. One would give much to know
just what rites were celebrated here, for though we have a
general notion of what Mithraism stood for, details are
hard to come by, especially as most of our informants were
Christians, who were naturally prejudiced witnesses.

This temple was destroyed by the barbarians in 296, but
it was soon rebuilt at a higher level. Nave and aisles were
separated by timber pillars and in the sanctuary three altars
to Mithras were set up at different times side by side, by
prefects of the local cohort. It is interesting to note that one
of these hailed from Italy, another from the Rhineland and
that the third may be an officer who later served as a district governor in Egypt. One of these altars had a representation of the demi-god, his face and torso painted white,
with a scarlet cloak about his shoulders and a halo pierced
along its rays for lighting from behind. In addition, statues
of the two torch-bearers, Cautes and Cautopates, standing
with their legs crossed, were erected. The temple was finally

abandoned when some interference with the stream flowing
along the hollow here flooded the site. But before it collapsed the statues of the two torch-bearers were deliberately destroyed, though the three altars were undamaged.
The excavators suggested that this may have been the result
of orders from a Christian commandant, but we shall never
know.

Retracing our steps towards the road, but keeping in the
hollow, we come to a reedy swamp and, just over a stone
wall, what looks like a well half hidden by wild forget-me-
nots. This is all that now remains of Coventina's Well. A
few centuries ago the surrounding masonry could be seen
and the folk there called it 'the cold bath'. In 1876 John
Clayton's attention was drawn to the structure, which had
been rediscovered by some miners prospecting for lead. He
excavated the site, with remarkable results. For he found a
jumble of stones, altars and inscriptions, and beneath these
the foundations of a temple forty feet by thirty-eight internally, which he dated to Antoninus Pius. In the midst of this
was the well, then seven feet deep. The greatest surprise
was a hoard of coins, of which Clayton recovered over thirteen thousand after visitors had wantonly made off with
many more. Now in the Black Gate at Newcastle, they
ranged from Mark Antony to Gratian, murdered in 383, at
least, the most numerous dating from Trajan to Marcus
Aurelius in the second century. Clearly this was the shrine
of the deity of the spring, with a sacred well into which the
pious had poured their votive offerings through the centuries. Clearly, too, it had suffered a violent end, when
temple and shrine had been suddenly wrecked and the
débris thrown contemptuously into the well, unless the
votaries had entrusted their treasures to the keeping of the
goddess, hoping to return. Altars and votive tablets, many
of which are in Chesters Museum, showed that the deity
was the water nymph Coventina, who is otherwise unknown in the Empire. Some think her name is Celtic, others
Greek, others again that her cult was brought here by the

Aquitanians who first occupied the fort. One tablet, set up by the prefect of the Batavian cohort, shows her reclining gracefully on a large water-lily leaf and holding a branch: another has her in triplicate under three arches, or it may be with two attendant nymphs: two altars to her were inscribed in faulty Latin by two Germans, and another inscription, dedicated by the Cugernian cohort, witnesses to the continued popularity of the nymph with successive contingents. There is something appealing about little Coventina – 'sole goddess of this desolation' – no deity with wide powers over vast supernatural spheres like Jupiter or Mars, but content to preside faithfully over this meagre stream, while nevertheless winning such devoted allegiance from these rough soldiers. Have we, who turn our water-taps unthinkingly, become so utilitarian that we have lost our sense of poetry and forgotten our dependence on the forces of nature? Or were Coventina's worshippers sunk in superstition? Were they not, rather, groping for something which our fathers since won but which we, almost choked in material amenities, are in danger of throwing away? We still have our superstitions, for all that, for I was told that modern pilgrims still cast their sixpences, and even half-crowns, into her well.

Leaving Carrawburgh, I continued along the road, the Wall ditch here being filled with king-cups. I passed Milecastle 32 on the left and then No 33 (Shield on the Wall), its outlines showing up well in the hay. Farther on, a reservoir, looking like a natural mere and crowned by a graceful plantation beyond, added a welcome splash of colour after the rather drab surroundings of Carrawburgh. Better still was the sight in front of me – the Whin Sill which rises from south to north in successive waves and then drops suddenly in a long escarpment to the rolling plain to the north. Seen from east or west, these ridges have a fascinating appearance, often likened to gigantic waves throwing themselves on a shelving shore. It is along their crests that the Wall is soon to climb so magnificently, yet so calmly, as if such

hazards were positively welcomed, to show what its intrepid builders could accomplish.

The road descends slightly to cross a small burn, the
Coesike, and then, *mirabile dictu*, veers slightly to the left,
allowing the Wall to climb alone up the edge of the first
crest. From here almost to Birdoswald we are done with
roads, which mercifully could not face the ups and downs of
the crags, so that we can follow our Wall in freedom along
its grandest stretch, where it clings to the summit of the
escarpment, running forward with the headlands and re-
treating in the gaps. The Vallum likewise remains below,
between the Wall and the road, while between Vallum and
Wall the Roman Military Way can be seen all along this
sector. We can follow any one of these works according to
our inclination, but the pilgrim worth his salt will choose the
roughest way and stick to the Wall.

It was good to be off the road, but it was slower going on
the grass and the crags. From the burn the Wall climbs
steadily past Sewingshields Farm, to build which it was
extensively robbed. But the ditch is very clear, until at
Milecastle 34, in a plantation, it ends for the time being.
The cliffs dropping to the north were sufficient defence and
for many miles onwards we shall only see occasional small
lengths of it, where the cliff disappears for a stretch. Turning south, I had a fine view of the Vallum, here going off at
an angle from the Wall somewhat to the south.

Just below the farm is the site of Sewingshields Castle,
where tradition said that King Arthur and his court were
held prisoner by an enchantment until someone should
blow a bugle and cut a garter with a sword, all of which lay
handy on a table. None could find the entrance until the
farmer of Sewingshields, knitting near by, dropped his ball
of thread, which fell into the overgrown passage-way. Following the clue, he penetrated into a vast hall where king,
queen and courtiers reclined entranced. He took the sword
and cut the garter, whereat the recumbent figures slowly
rose, but the 'witless wight' was so scared that he fled with-

out blowing the indispensable bugle. So Arthur and his peers still await their disenchantment. I could do nothing to help them, for I could see only a pattern of low mounds, in a field, with a line of bright stones parallel to the Wall. Passing through a plantation of firs, I came to the basaltic columns which grace the edge of the precipice. When William Hutton was here, he was taken by the farmer to sit in what he called 'King Ethel's Chair' set in a chimney-like rock on the edge of the cliff. This should, of course, be 'King Arthur's Chair', but it has since been deliberately thrown down by a rustic.

I had now reached the summit, nearly 1,100 feet above sea level, following the Wall along the edge of the precipice. Below, I could see the first of the group of loughs which un-expectedly beautify the moorland scene about here, that of Broomlee, lying darkly amidst the treeless grass. Hutton found all this depressing. 'A more dreary country than this in which I now am, can scarcely be conceived. I do not wonder it shocked Camden. The country itself would frighten him without the Troopers'. For it was just beyond here, where the Wall descends to Busy Gap, that Camden and Robert Cotton had to break off their journey in 1599. 'I could not with safety take the full survey of it, for the rank robbers thereabouts'.

These 'Busy Gap rogues' had long been infamous for their maraudings, but in the latter part of the sixteenth century the Armstrongs and their allies conducted a veritable private war which held all the lonelier parts of the North to ransom. Secure in their headquarters on Tarras Moor be-tween Esk and Liddell, they exploited the agelong Border unrest to raid at will, driving off cattle and horses, which they exchanged for good Scotch whisky, and even kidnap-ping hapless Englishmen. When the union of the realms seemed imminent, they did their best to embroil Anglo-Scottish relations and in 1596 actually released one of their lairds from Carlisle prison. Elizabeth I tried the expedient of a dual commission to assess damages on both sides: the

English losses were found to amount to £54,000 and the
Scottish to £10,000, but not a penny could be extracted.
James VI was powerless, but finally the Queen's cousin, Sir
Robert Carey, swept Tarras and, though many of the
Armstrongs escaped his net, their power was broken. Two
years later James ascended the English throne and the
Borders found comparative tranquillity.

After Busy Gap the Wall climbs again to Milecastle 36
and then, after further ups and downs, and skirting a plantation, we descend to the broad valley through which flows
the Knag Burn. On the heights beyond is Housesteads. At
Knag Burn was a gate through the Wall, probably built in
the fourth century, the only one known beside that at Portgate and, of course, those in the forts and milecastles. The
guard-houses on each side can be still seen, a few feet high.
I was glad to reach Housesteads, for it was now half past
five and it seemed that I must once more do without tea or
any substitute. But the guardian of the fort found me some
lime-juice and biscuits, which I devoured in the vestibule of
the museum. The former was certainly the best drink I had
had for a long time, having gone so long without any. I then
made a preliminary tour of the fort and museum, and
decided to return for a further exploration on Monday. For

Gold medallion commemorating recovery of Britain and
liberation of London by Constantius Chlorus

I still had a long walk down to and across the Military Road and then up and down again to Bardon Mill. Here I just caught a train, with no time to get a ticket, and so back to Corbridge. Bath and dinner were specially welcome that night, after a long but enjoyable day, with very meagre rations. I should, of course, have put up for the night near Housesteads, but I was comfortable at the 'Golden Lion' and tomorrow was Sunday. Housesteads, then, must wait for the next chapter.

9

CHESTERHOLM: HOUSESTEADS TO GREATCHESTERS

Majestic though in ruins.
MILTON, *Paradise Lost*, II, 305

After three fine days Sunday was disappointing. Once more it was raining with that purposeful persistence so common in the north and everything was wrapped in grey monotones. I made my way – waded would be apter – to the parish church, where there was a good congregation in spite of the excuse offered by the weather to the half-hearted. Corbridge church, dedicated to St Andrew, should be examined by the Wall pilgrim. Its Saxon tower, with a seventh-century porch, embodies an arch clearly taken from a Roman gateway, presumably from Corstopitum. Lewis holes can be seen in some of the stones. The nave has a Saxon core, with an arcade of about 1200, and the thirteenth-century chancel is graced with three tall narrow lancets at its eastern end.

The familiar words and ceremonies of the Prayer Book struck me with new force after my week's encounter with so many old pagan cults and my efforts to get inside the minds of their adherents. The lukewarm Christian, or those who think that it does not matter what a man believes so long as his conduct is satisfactory, might do worse than make a study of paganism in the Roman Empire. They might discover that the Church, after all, has treasures which these others lacked. Jupiter might lead men to some conception of the All-Father, Mars might inspire courage (but more likely revenge), Coventina and her like might clothe Nature with poetry. Marcus Aurelius shows us what philosophy could do for the best characters, Lucius in the *Golden Ass* the appeal of the mystery religions. But what are all these beside the tremendous declaration 'I am the Resurrection and the Life'? Which of them, for that matter, told men that 'Now abideth Faith, Hope and *Caritas*, but the greatest of these is *Caritas*'? Augustine found much help from pagan cults and philosophy in his search for God, but nowhere, he declares, did he read that 'The Word was made flesh'. The New Testament, it may be remembered, is one of the source documents of Roman history, and the rise of Christianity one of the major episodes in the story of the Empire.

Not that these pagan cults should be despised. Had not Christianity arisen when it did, who knows what the process of syncretism already at work might not have achieved in a fusion of the best in the mystery religions with the highest philosophy? Christianity itself was an oriental cult, more refined, no doubt, and boasting what these others never claimed, a basis in historic fact: but it worked on human hearts by much the same means. Its early assemblies were humble affairs, without elaborate ritual or gorgeous vestments, but they were more akin to the mysteries than to a Quaker or Salvation Army meeting, for their essence was the worship of God in prayer and sacrament, to which preaching was but an adjunct.

When Hadrian built his Wall, Christianity had already grown from a small eastern sect into a federation of local churches established in most of the urban centres around the Mediterranean. Each church was governed by its bishop, assisted by a handful of priests and deacons, ministering to lowly congregations. This empire-wide organization, as well as the fervour of the early believers, enabled the Church not only to survive outlawry and intermittent persecution, but to grow, until by the third century it was becoming clear that the Christians must be liquidated if they were not to capture or at least disrupt the Empire. So there followed the persecutions of Decius, Valerian and Diocletian, and, when these failed, the conversion of Constantine and his grant of toleration to all religions. To many, the official adoption of Christianity has seemed the worst blow suffered by the Church. Henceforth the hypocrites and the lukewarm were on the Christian side, with depressing effect on the spiritual life of the Church. Soon, too, the Church would be only too willing to enlist the support of the state which had once persecuted her. In vain would that staunch pagan Symmachus plead *Uno itinere non potest pervenire ad tam grande secretum.* Yet only so could be launched the mighty and not ignoble task of building a Christian civilization. Either way there was loss and gain. Either the Church could remain a purely spiritual society, ministering to the elect and almost abandoning the world to the devil, or she could embrace the world and endeavour to spiritualize the whole social fabric. Her adoption of the second course produced the glories, as well as the defects, of medieval Christendom.

We know nothing of the coming of Christianity to Britain. The legends which bring Joseph of Arimathea, and even some of the Apostles, to Britain will be swallowed only by the gullible, but they may conceal traditions of its early arrival here. Tertullian, early in the third century, claimed that parts of Britain unreached by Roman arms had been conquered for Christ: later writers record the names of St Alban and of two others, the first British martyrs: and we know that British bishops attended church councils on the Continent in 314 and 359. Small Christian churches have been found at Silchester and Lullingstone, and what looks like one at Caerwent. On the other hand, paganism was still flourishing and even reviving in the fourth century.

There are few traces of Christianity around the Wall, for the cities were its chief centres. No Christian inscription like *Soror, ave, vivas in Deo*, from York, can be matched further north. A silver cup from Corbridge bore the Chi-

Rho symbol, the first two letters of the name of Christ in Greek, but there is little more. Probably few Roman Britons, especially in the north, sang the hymns of Ambrose or Prudentius, or that lovely

> O lux beata Trinitas,
> et principalis Unitas,
> iam sol recedit igneus,
> infunde lumen cordibus.
>
> Te mane laudum carmine,
> Te deprecamur vespere,
> Te nostra supplex gloria
> per cuncta laudet saecula.

Yet before the fourth century was out St Ninian was converting the heathen beyond the Wall, and soon after Roman rule ended all Britain was nominally Christian. Clearly the faith must have made great strides in the previous century, but details are entirely lacking. We know that one of the last provincial governors was a Christian and that there was a bishop at York. Is it fanciful to envisage the latter sending out missions to the north which, encouraged perhaps by a friendly governor or local commandant, began the conversion of the folk around the Wall? History is silent, yet it is clear that when at last Rome withdrew her garrisons she was already reaching out to build the foundations of a new but spiritual empire.

After a hasty lunch, I said goodbye to Corbridge for good and caught the bus westward. The rain was as persistent as ever, but by the time I got off at Bardon Mill it had mercifully stopped. My pack felt heavy as I climbed the stiff hill, but there was reward in the vista which rose and expanded to the south as I climbed. It brought to mind that passage of Alice Meynell, describing the climber: 'You lift the world, you raise the horizon . . . like the scene in the Vatican when a cardinal, with his dramatic Italian

hands, bids the kneeling groups to arise. He does more than
bid them. He lifts them, he gathers them up, far and near
... with the compulsion of his expressive force ... You are
but a man lifting his weight upon the upward road, but as
you climb the circle of the world goes up to face you.' The
weather was now clearing, occasional pale gleams of sun lit
up the clumps of golden broom, and a lark or two sang
cheerfully overhead. One is soon in a new world, cut off
from the villages and villas in the valley with Barcombe
Hill rising steeply on the right.

Near this hill were several Roman quarries, in one of
which a labourer named Thomas Pattinson found a bronze
arm-purse in 1837, containing three gold and sixty silver
Roman coins, ranging from Claudius to Hadrian. Hoping
to cash in on his find, Thomas refused to hand it over to the
Duke of Northumberland, on whose land it was found, and
toured the neighbourhood looking for a generous bidder.
Eventually he was sent to prison for a year and long after
his death purse and coins were bought from his brother by
John Clayton for fifty pounds. They are now in Chesters
Museum.

I took a grassy path which forked left off the road and so
came to Chesterholm: but I found I had gone through
private property, and the visitor had better keep to the road
until he reaches the lane which branches to his left. We are
now on the Stanegate. As we make for the fort we pass a
Roman milestone in its original position. The fort itself
occupies a slight plateau just west of the Chineley Burn and
south of a tributary, being well defended by nature on all
sides but the west. Built by Agricola, it was called Vindo-
lana, apparently meaning the 'white close', and covered
three and a half acres. It was destroyed by the invaders of
197, rebuilt early in the third century, and again destroyed
in 296, after which Constantius Chlorus replanned it and
reduced its length by redrawing its north and south walls.
Its garrison in the third and fourth centuries was the
Fourth Cohort of Gauls, whose movements are better

known than those of any other auxiliary unit on or near the Wall. In Hadrian's time it was at Templeborough in Yorkshire, then at Castlesteads farther west on the Wall: about 180 it moved to Risingham on Dere Street, and soon after to Castlehill on Antonine's Wall. Chesterholm may meanwhile have been occupied by the Third Cohort of Nervians.

The site has been acquired and excavated by Mr Eric Birley, who has done so much to enlarge our knowledge of Roman antiquities in the North. The walls of the fort, its north gate and the headquarters are exposed, under the care of the Ministry of Works. The north gate, with guard-houses on each side, stands nine courses high, but the *principia* is the best relic here. Built by Constantius and reconstructed by Count Theodosius, it has the usual features, but here they can be studied better than perhaps anywhere else. The central hall has several decorated slabs and the tribunal stands at its western end. Behind the westernmost of the five rooms can be seen the short pillars of a hypocaust, with a drain. In front of the building are two verandahs which, with most of the rooms flanking the courtyard and the offices on each side of the 'chapel', were converted into storehouses by Theodosius. Under this were found the remains of the third-century headquarters, facing south, whereas the fourth-century fort faced north.

Among inscriptions found at Chesterholm is a fine altar, now in Chesters Museum, erected by Pituanius Secundus, prefect of the Gaulish cohort, to the Genius of the Prae-torium, or commandant's house, in which it was found. On one side are depicted the sacrificial victim, an ox, with axe and knife for its slaughter: on the other a jug and a dish for pouring a libation of wine. Another altar, to Jupiter and the other gods and the Genius of the Praetorium, was set up by another prefect from Italy. At Housesteads, too, is a testi-monial of the loyalty of the Gauls here to Caracalla. Another inscription records the restoration from the foun-dations of a gate and towers by Claudius Xenophon, governor of Lower Britain in 223. Severus, it should be noted, had divided Britain into two provinces, Upper and Lower Britain, the boundary between which is only vaguely known. Under Diocletian, Britain was made a diocese, subject to the Prefect of Gaul, and divided into four, and later five, provinces.

Just west of the fort are the remains of the bath house, now showing as grassy hummocks, to which water was brought by a conduit from a spring near by. Farther west still was the usual *vicus*, notable here for an altar, now in Chesters Museum, erected to the divinity of the Emperors and to Vulcan by the *vicani vindolandenses*, that is, by the settlement as a corporate entity. We have similar evidence for the *vici* at Housesteads and at Old Carlisle, showing that even there, and presumably elsewhere, these humble villages had their due place in the Roman constitution. Just what their powers were and how they managed their affairs we can only guess. No doubt it was a very slightly glorified parish pump: yet here, as in the towns, were the germs of self-government, which might with encouragement have led to great things. Unfortunately, circumstances only made for increasing autocracy at the centre of the Empire and political liberty was finally extinguished.

There are signs that the fort met its end by burning. The date is uncertain, but a coin of Valentinian II (389–92), one of those later than 383 found near the Wall, suggests that it survived the generally-accepted date for the withdrawal of the Wall garrison, or may support the thesis that that withdrawal was later than 383. The civil settlement probably survived still longer, as a tombstone inscribed *Brigomaglos iacit [qui et Brioc]us* (now at Chesters), is clearly Christian and from the fifth century. This person is thought to be a Briton of that name who worked with St Germanus in Gaul.

Leaving Chesterholm, I walked westwards along the Stanegate. On the way I passed the base of another Roman milestone, the missing portion of which had an inscription in honour of an Emperor. Turning right at the cross-roads and crossing a pleasant burn, I at last regained the Military Road some two miles west of Housesteads and made for the 'Bognor' Guest House, where I had booked accommodation. Here I found a welcome 'plain tea', consisting of toasted and buttered tea cake, white and brown bread-and-butter with crabapple jelly, home-made cakes and a slice of apple pie. Mrs Ridley, who provides appetizing meals like that at all times, told me that the bungalow was built by her father-in-law for his retirement in 1929, when King George V was convalescing at Bognor (hence the name), but that they had so many hungry and benighted ramblers clamouring for refreshment and shelter that the place virtually turned itself into a guest house. For the Military Road here runs through a shallow valley, just south of the Wall, almost bereft of habitations, through which a few cars scamper as if frightened by the brooding loneliness. The Vallum, which has followed the lower ground between the Wall and the Military Road for some miles, approached the road a mile back, which has since been running along its south berm. Just before the 'Bognor' it again bends north and runs through Mrs Ridley's back garden.

Just near are the 'Twice Brewed' Inn and the 'Once Brewed', now a youth hostel, but otherwise there are only a few scattered farms. At the old 'Twice Brewed' to the east, now a farm, William Hutton obtained a bed in 1801, after much persuasion, but had to sup with a troop of carriers, who ate a piece of beef out of the copper perhaps equal to half a calf, followed by a pudding as big as a peck measure. Each piece that went down their throats, as if there were no barricade, was more than a moderate man would eat at one whole meal, he says. 'They convinced me that eating was the chief end of man.'

Later I took a stroll, but soon returned, for it was quickly dark and really cold. I was glad to see a fire in the lounge and not sorry, though surprised, to find a hot bottle in my bed. Mrs Ridley's motherly care certainly pampers the pilgrim who aspires to make a tough expedition. There have been Ridleys in these parts for centuries and we shall presently pass the seat of John Ridley, brother of the Marian martyr. One young Ridley – John Graham, a nephew – not quite eleven, is an enthusiastic Wall 'fan'. He reeled off the names of all its forts, in English and Latin and in the right order, and could quote whole chunks from Bruce-Richmond and Miss Mothersole. I told him that he was suffering from Ro-mania, but it was good to encounter such keenness: he had even read reports from *Archaeologia Aeliana*!

'D'you know what the Romans made their mortar from?' he asked me.

'Mostly limestone,' I began.

'No. Limestone and water and – blood!'

'Blood?' I queried: 'what sort of blood?'

'Oh, animals' blood: or else they just caught a Pict and cut off his head and poured the blood out,' illustrating the process with appropriate gestures.

Next morning, Monday June 21st, I resumed my interrupted tour of the Wall at Housesteads. This fort may be called the *pièce de résistance* of Hadrian's Wall, for it occupies the finest natural site and has been better preserved than any other. I was fortunate to light upon Dr D. J. Smith, also staying at the 'Bognor', who was then in charge of current excavations on this site and who gladly answered my thirst for information.

The *Notitia* calls the fort Borcovicium, but this is now regarded as incorrect, since an inscription shows that its name began with Ver-. Its garrison in the third and fourth centuries was the First Cohort of Tungrians, from the district around Tongres in Belgic Gaul. Inscriptions suggest that it was also occupied in the second century by a detachment of the Second Legion and that in the third its garrison was reinforced by a *cuneus Frisiorum*, or Frisian cavalry, and by the *numerus Hnaudifridi*, an irregular infantry unit commanded or raised by one Notfried, presumably a German. The fort is four and three-quarters miles from Carrawburgh and covered just over five acres. It was given in 1930 by Mr J. M. Clayton to the National Trust, to which Dr G. M. Trevelyan also presented the nearby farm and surrounding land.

Its site is magnificent. The north wall of the fort lies along the edge of the Whin Sill escarpment, which here drops steeply nearly a hundred feet. Southward, the ground slopes slightly at first and then steeply, while on the east it falls sharply to the Knag Burn. The fort was laid out on the usual plan, with four double gateways, each provided with towers and guard-houses, and the usual headquarters building, commandant's house, barracks and granaries: but at Housesteads the foundations of all these features can be seen exposed, with the surrounding walls, giving us a nearer approximation to the original picture than can be obtained elsewhere. It should be noticed at the outset that the fort is exceptional, though not unique, in having its long axis running parallel to the Wall, because of the narrow ledge on which it was built.

There is no need to take the visitor round the fort in detail, since we have done this at other forts and he can easily find his way with the help of the Guide obtainable at the adjoining museum and the notices at each structure. Only the salient features need to be pointed out here. First, it should be noted how the narrow Wall joins the fort at its north-east and north-west corners. At the former the original angle-tower had been replaced by another a few yards to the west, to fit the junction with the narrow Wall, which was therefore later than the fort. But the fort itself was later than the broad Wall, for the foundations of the latter and of Turret 36B had already been laid and were covered by the rampart of the fort and by the road just behind it. One portal of each gate was later blocked up, on the north almost at once. At the east gate the blocked southern portal became a guard-house and the old guard-house was used to store coal, a supply of which was found by the excavators.

On the west the other portal was also blocked in the reconstruction by Theodosius. The imposing north gate looks supremely useless, but it led to an inclined road, removed by Clayton when excavating, down which troops and supplies could pass without too much difficulty. There were interval towers between those of the gates, added probably by Constantius.

The headquarters, which here faces east, was on the usual plan. The foundations now visible are of the Severan building. Its forecourt was flanked by verandahs, the water from the eaves of which dripped into a gutter still visible. In the last days of the fort these verandahs, and the central hall, were converted into living rooms, while in the northernmost of the five rooms at the rear arrow-heads were manufactured. Some eight hundred of these were found by the excavators, suggesting that, as danger increased, armourers became more important than accountants.

Immediately north of the headquarters was the granary, converted later into a double range, the pillars from under the floors of which still stand. These, too, in the last period were turned into living rooms, changes which are thought to indicate the withdrawal of the civil population, or at least the troops' families, within the fort by Theodosius. South of the headquarters was the commandant's house, with his private bath building to its west. Behind, that is, west of, the headquarters was a building, no foundations of which are now visible, which has been identified as the hospital and sick-bay. The rest of the fort area – the *praetentura* east of the *via principalis* joining the north and south gates and the *retentura* west of the parallel *via quintana* – was mainly occupied by barracks. There are six parallel blocks in each of these front and rear sections of the fort, but as the garrison was here one thousand strong and allowing one century to each block, two must have been used for other purposes, such as workshops.

The latrine was just west of the south-east angle-tower,

Model of Housesteads Fort by W. Bulmer, Esq, Hon Keeper,
Corbridge Museum

Top: Housesteads. The north granary from the north-west.
Bottom: Housesteads. The latrine and cisterns from the west

Top: Housesteads. The West Gate from the east.
Bottom: Remains of Milecastle 39, at Castle Nick. *From a painting by H. B. Richardson, 1848, in the Laing Art Gallery, Newcastle*

Bust of Septimius Severus. *British Museum*

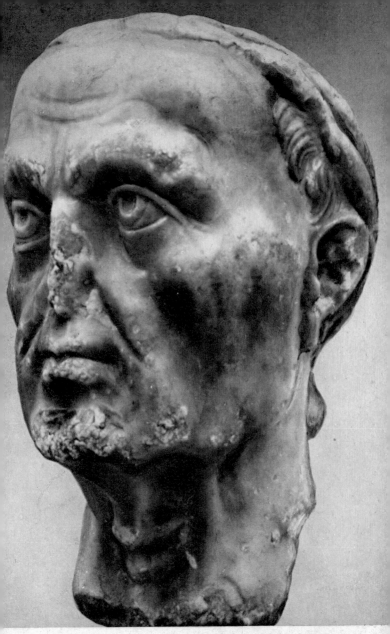

Alabaster head of Constantius Chlorus. *British Museum*

Top: Hadrian's Wall looking east towards Housesteads.
Bottom: Panorama looking over Birdoswald along Hadrian's Wall, which runs alongside the road. The Turf Wall and Vallum are to the left of the wall; the river Irthing can be seen in the bottom left-hand corner. Looking west

Top: Part of the depot at Corbridge, from the air, showing the store-house (Site XL), granaries and, beyond the road, the temples and two military compounds. *Bottom:* The abutment at Willowford Bridge

Sepulchral slab from Carlisle. *Tullie House, Carlisle*

with a sewer passing under the fort wall to emerge a hundred yards away. This, curiously enough, is perhaps the most interesting feature now visible. It consisted of a long room with a line of seats over a sewer on each side. These are now covered by turf, but the central stone passage which separated them is still there, with a channel each side, in front of where the seats were, down which water for washing sponges (toilet paper not having been invented) ran from a large tank, still standing, its joints still filled with lead. At the end of the passage is a stone basin for washing the hands. The complicated stone channels along which the water ran are evidence of the care taken by the Romans in these matters, neglected for long afterwards. Somewhat similar arrangements existed in some medieval monasteries, and Elizabeth I's godson, Sir John Harington, sketched a somewhat playful idea of a water-closet, but it was not until the nineteenth century that the question was seriously tackled.

To supply the fort with water must have presented a greater problem here than at most other forts on the Wall. It has been surmised that water may have been pumped up from the burn, but the Romans took no chances and several tanks to collect rainwater were built. The troops' bath house lay just east of the Knag Burn, but it has not yet been excavated, much having been destroyed by robbing and by floods.

It will be remembered that in the fourth century there was a gate in the Wall at Knag Burn. Apparently there was also a village here. But the main civil settlement was on the slope to the south and west of the fort, one of the largest outside a Wall station, the lingering remains of which gave the place its name. Here buildings sprang up in the third century on each side of the road running south from the south gate of the fort and over the Vallum by the usual crossing. Another road skirted the south-east angle of the fort and crossed the first road in a line gradually diverging from the fort's south wall. Excavations have not proceeded further, but it is thought that the settlement may have covered some eight acres. The villagers apparently lived partly by trade through the Knag Burn gateway, for there was considerable commerce between Roman Britain and the Caledonians, partly by supplying the garrison with necessities, and partly by growing corn in the fields on the slopes of the hill, where the outlines of regular terraces can still be seen.

Several of these houses, mostly half-timber on a stone foundation, were substantial buildings over fifty feet by twenty. No 8 (the number of the site, not, of course, the Roman address), some distance down the southward road on its eastern side, was a shop or tavern and has achieved fame as the 'murder house'. For under its clay floor were found the skeletons of a man and a woman, whose burial there and not in the cemetery beyond the settlement showed that they had met untimely deaths: the point of a sword was still lodged in the man's ribs. Building No 5, on the opposite side of the road and nearest the fort, and No 7 farther south, were constructed of better masonry and have been thought to have been designed for some official purpose, at present unknown. Other dwellings here were of the meanest type. Clearly the population was very mixed, ranging from officials and time-expired soldiers to natives in varying stages of romanization.

Beyond these houses were several temples and shrines, affording almost as much choice of religions as at Corbridge. These included a Mithraeum, situate in the valley beyond the farmhouse. It was forty-two feet by sixteen internally, with a smaller shrine at one end. From this came a fine statue of Mithras slaying the bull, a bust of him surrounded by the signs of the zodiac and pierced for lighting from behind, two altars to him, and statues of his two torch-bearers. One of these altars was erected by a *beneficiarius consularis*, a legionary seconded for police duty, probably at the Knag Burn gateway; and if so, testifying to the importance of the trading station there. Also honoured here

was Mars Thincsus, another example of the fusion of barbarian and Roman deities, shown accompanied by pairs of
Valkyries, called Alaisiagae, on monuments erected by the
Frisian units mentioned above. Here, too, were found dedications to godlings called Hueter and Cocidius, popular
from here to the western end of the Wall, a fine statue of
the Mothers, a German cult imported by the troops, and
three curious deities in hooded cloaks, also apparently imported and thought by some to be prototypes of the dwarfs
who figure in later legend. They look curiously like three
grandmothers caught in the rain. A statue of Nemesis, set
up by a priest called Apollonius, apparently an oriental,
suggests that she had a temple here. An altar shows Hercules wrestling with the Nemaean lion and on its sides the
Lernean hydra and the garden of the Hesperides. A dedication to the 'gods and goddesses' was set up in obedience
to an oracle delivered by Apollo in Ionia. There is also an
interesting tombstone to Anicius Ingenuus, aged twenty-
five, a surgeon (*medicus*) serving in the ranks with the
Tungrian cohort. He would be a private with a special func-
tion, in this case medical, or probably merely 'first aid'.
Medicine was not one of the higher professions in Roman
days. Most of these monuments are now in the museums at
Newcastle or Chesters, but some, including Hercules and
the hooded deities, are in that by the fort here.

Cocidius, the local godling mentioned above, was also
honoured at many forts west of Housesteads and also in
some of the northern outpost forts. In the eastern part of
the area where his cult was thus popular, he is often
equated with Silvanus, the Roman patron of hunters, like St
Hubert in later days, while farther west he is often identified with Mars. Professor Richmond suggests that this
shows that the eastern sector of this area was more settled
than the district farther west in Roman times. Cocidius is
represented rather grotesquely on a silver plaque found at
Bewcastle, which rather provokes one to attempt a limerick
on the lines of

There was an old man called Cocidius,
Whose features were perfectly hideous ...

but perhaps this is best left to the reader to complete, if he
likes that sort of thing.

Housesteads Museum has many other exhibits of great
interest. The visitor who has time might well call there before exploring the fort and *vicus*, for Mr Bulmer's realistic
reconstructions of the fort, of the west gate and of a typical
house in the village will enable him to follow more imag-
inatively what he sees outside. He should then return for a
lengthier study of the minor objects. These include a fine
'Samian' bowl, a cooking jar of local ware, a pipe-clay
statuette of Venus, brooches, signet rings containing gems,
bronze and iron *stili* for writing and bone hairpins and
needles. There is an iron sickle and part of a flail, no doubt
once used on the terraces outside. Numerous photographs
show the results of excavations no longer visible on the
ground.

Leaving Housesteads, I embarked on what is easily the
most attractive and probably the best known sector of the
Wall. Passing through a thin plantation, we keep along the
edge of the precipice, with Greenlee Lough, the largest of
the local 'lakes', shimmering in the wastes to the north.
Looking back, one has a fine view of the Wall descending
to Knag Burn, with Broomlee Lough beyond, while to the
south Grindon Lough is seen. The Wall is preserved to a
fair height all the way here and one can walk on it, as well
as beside it, if one wishes.

It was the longest day of the year, but there was nothing
to suggest 'flaming June'. The early rain had now stopped,
but it was still overcast and unseasonably cold. However, I
decided to ignore the weather and was soon rewarded with
something a little more genial. A quarter of a mile from the
fort I came to Housesteads Milecastle, No 37. Its north
wall, standing to twenty-one courses, or over ten feet, and
its north gate, are better preserved than in any other ex-

ample. This wall is the usual broad gauge, tapering to the narrow gauge on each side. The gateway was arched at each end – the springers can still be seen, as well as several stones of the arch on the ground, with lewis holes in them. An inscription showed that the milecastle was built by the Second Legion under A. Platorius Nepos. It was badly damaged in 197 and its arches broken down: these were not restored under Severus, and the double gateway, ten feet wide, was reduced to a single portal of four feet. It looks as if here, at least, the original builders had slavishly followed their blueprint without considering its usefulness in face of the precipice beyond. One can still see how the invaders threw the jambs of the gateway out of perpendicular. The foundations of stone buildings can be seen in the eastern half of the milecastle, presumably for the commander and NCOs, the privates being housed in a timber block in the other half.

Presently the Wall descends down Housesteads Crags into the first of the many gaps which break up the escarpment. These are always delightful, as one watches the structure, like some huge snake, descending and climbing so triumphantly and wonders what scenes were enacted when the gangs of legionaries tackled their formidable task undaunted by the hazards set them by Nature. One wonders, too, what impression it made on the beholders when at last completed in all its new brightness. Did they realize the utter contrast between this neat, man-made structure and the untamed wildness all around? More likely they were only interested in wine, women and song – plus gambling. Poor old Hutton found it heavy going here. 'I now had the severe task of creeping up rocks and climbing stone walls, not well adapted to a man who has lost the activity of youth.'

Thence we climb at once to Cuddy's Crag, whose name is said to commemorate St Cuthbert's activities hereabouts in the seventh century, down again to Rapishaw Gap, and up once more to Hotbank Crags, which rise to 1074 feet.

Looking back from these last two heights, we enjoy the oft-pictured views to the plantation at Housesteads and the crests of Sewingshields. Ahead, we catch our first glimpse of Crag Lough and, looking round, discover that all four loughs are now in sight. Immediately to the south the Vallum shows up well and farther off Chesterholm can be made out below Barcombe Hill. In the distance are Tyne-dale and Allendale, with Cold Fell (2930 feet) outlined above them. On fine days one should also see the peaks of the Lake District far away, but I was not so lucky. I could, however, stretch my eyes northwards to rolling moors crowned by the distant Cheviots.

We descend from Hotbank to Milking Gap where, near the farm, the outline of Milecastle 38 can be traced by its stones, with some internal buildings. Two slabs recording its building by Platorius Nepos were found. We notice how the Wall bends south at the gap to form a re-entrant and thus enable the defenders to enfilade any attackers. Also that our old friend the ditch re-appears on the level ground. The Romans were taking no chances.

Climbing again, I passed through a delightful plantation overlooking Crag Lough. This is perhaps the prettiest of the lakes, graced by trees at one end and by reeds at the other, with waterhens and wild ducks swimming on its placid surface. At times swans also can be seen here: apparently they like to move from one lough to another. The precipice is here softened by a carpet of bracken amidst its rocks and patches of soft grass rich with wild flowers. No better spot could be wished for a brief lunch and a pipe, ensconced in a rocky projection, giving a delightful view through the firs over the lough to Hotbank Farm and the Wall descending beyond. Pale patches of sunlight ventured out, while overhead seagulls, jackdaws and an occasional curlew wheeled companionably. I had not met a single human since Housesteads and was left to whatever patrolling Romans and marauding Caledonians my imagination could conjure up.

Reluctantly tearing myself from this pleasant spot, I

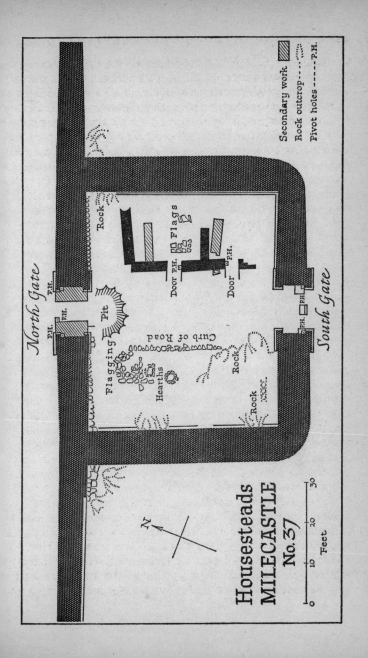

Housesteads
MILECASTLE
No. 37

North Gate

South Gate

Secondary work
Rock outcrop
Pivot holes — — — P.H.

Rock

Flags

Door P.H.

P.H.

Door

P.H.

P.H.

Flagging Pit

P.H.

P.H.

P.H.

Curb of Road

Rock

Hearths

Rock

Rock

N

0   10   20   30   Feet

passed Turret 28B poised precariously on the edge of a cliff jutting over the precipice. Then came another gap, so steep in the descent that the Wall is built with its course parallel to the horizon and not to the ground as elsewhere on slopes. Climbing again, the Wall becomes a mere jumble of stones for a time, but the crags are very fine, cut up into shapes resembling columns. Then comes another gap, as narrow as it is steep on both sides, in which Milecastle 38, known as Castle Nick, is seen, well preserved. Its walls rise to seven courses; its gate, here built of small stones as the site was too remote and high to bring up the usual larger masonry, had been reduced under Severus. Inside, on the west this time, are the foundations of the officers' quarters. Just to the south the Military Way is well seen, especially where it descends from the east.

I did not envy the troops condemned to guard this post, for it faces a ridge only a quarter of a mile to the north, blocking all further outlook, while southwards an extensive view is obtainable only through a narrow gap. But no doubt the auxiliaries, like most of their kind today, recked little of views provided their rations came along. Not that these would be exciting. Each man would be issued with meal, which he could make into bread or porridge, vegetables and rough red wine: but he might enliven these with tit-bits from the shops near the forts or do a little hunting or scrounging on his own. The Romans were not large meat-eaters and the troops are known to have complained loudly when corn was unobtainable and meat was issued instead. Those who grumbled at the meat ration during the Second World War might take heart by reflecting how much the Roman soldier accomplished without this luxury.

Not only was their food dull, by our standards, but, except when the war was 'hot', dullness must have been the general lot of the men on the Wall. We must remember, however, that folk then, except the upper classes in the cities, were used to dullness, though perhaps there was less of this in Roman days than before and for many centuries afterwards. This question of dullness is one that could profitably form the subject of a thesis for postgraduate researchers. What people thought and what they felt in bygone days are at least as important as what they ate or how they earned their living, subjects which have absorbed much investigation. When one thinks of the humdrum lives lived by most people for most of historic times, and still lived by millions in backward countries today, when one glances at the huge tomes which the Schoolmen compiled, or the heavy books of sermons, theology and uplift which made up most of the reading of seventeenth- and eighteenth-century people, or when one reflects that Lyly's *Euphues* was a bestseller with the 'bright young things' of Elizabeth I's days, one gets the impression that dullness reigned supreme even in western Europe until a century or little more ago. Think, for example, of the few heavy volumes which composed the library of the average educated man in the two centuries after the invention of printing, and compare these with our 'desert island discs'. Yet probably our researcher would tell us that most of the readers of these things actually enjoyed them. If so, can it be that boredom is a modern disease engendered by the very inventions which are designed to relieve it? Certainly it is unhistorical to imagine that earlier ages were bored by lack of amenities and amusements which they had never known and could not even imagine. Many of us got along nicely before radio was invented, but can hardly do without it once we have experienced it. Its lack certainly never worried Hadrian, nor did his legionaries sigh for a fag as they built the Wall. So perhaps it would all depend on what the troops were used to before they came to the forts and milecastles.

Ascending again, I came to Cat Stairs, a gash in the ridge filled with huge stones tumbled down from the Wall. I clambered down this to get a view of the precipice from below, its top adorned with queer chimney-like columns of basalt. This is Peel Crag, beyond which comes another gap, where the Wall again forms a re-entrant, very striking to the west, and the ditch reappears, to continue to the next milecastle. Crossing a road, I was haunted for a stretch by two curlews, which circled incessantly around me, uttering their curious, but presently monotonous, cries. Clearly they disliked my intrusion on their solitude. I had seen a car as I crossed the road, and a little before a rambler, making eastwards, the only one I encountered on the whole of my expedition: but otherwise I might have been the only person in Northumberland for all I could see. At this point Professor Richmond points out a stretch of Wall which has been destroyed and entirely rebuilt and instances similar examples at Throckley, Matfen Piers, Portgate and Plane-trees. It must be remembered that the destruction of 197 was so severe that the necessary rebuilding by Severus's lieutenants led early antiquaries to the conclusion that it was that Emperor who was the first builder of the Wall, Hadrian's share being wrongly confined to the Vallum.

While the Wall-pilgrim is in this neighbourhood he can make a pleasant diversion, if he has time, by exploring the 'Northumberland Lake District'. These little loughs are rather insignificant, but they have a certain charm. We have already obtained a good view of Crag Lough just below the Wall: the others are more distant. To reach Greenlee Lough, the largest, one should take the road which turns north at the 'Once Brewed' Youth Hostel and follow it through Peel Gap in the Wall until it descends where a track sign-posted 'Bonnyrigg Hall' bends sharp to the right. This climbs a ridge to the left and descends to a farm, where it turns right to skirt a plantation. Soon after it passes the Hall, Greenlee is suddenly revealed below us to the north, its farther shore fringed by a thin line of trees, beyond which are a few scattered farms, while eastwards the upthrown waves of the limestone hills are silhouetted against the sky. This placid lough is worth visiting, not only for its quiet beauty but because all the way there one obtains the best view of the vertical-ribbed crags along which the Wall runs in this, the most magnificent part of its course. It needs little imagination to clothe them with Wall, milecastles and turrets in all their original splendour and to realize what an impression of the might of Rome they must have given the barbarians viewing them from the north. It is said that the water lilies on Greenlee are always white, those on Crag Lough yellow.

From Greenlee the traveller can continue to Broomlee Lough, the highest and bleakest of these lakes. Or if he cares for a longer expedition he can follow the stream north-eastwards from Greenlee to two lesser tarns, Folly Lake, the smallest of all, and Halleypike Lough. From the latter he can either regain the Wall and the Military Road, or if he feels energetic can continue to Simonburn on the North Tyne.

I was soon climbing again, for all this sector is like a switchback. This time it was to the highest point attained by the Wall in its whole course, at Winshields, 1230 feet above the sea. On clear days the view is enchanting, embracing Skiddaw, Criffell peaks beyond the Solway and the Cheviots, but, alas, the weather played me false: the sky had clouded since my sunlit lunch above Crag Lough, and by the time I reached the summit of Winshields I was shrouded in mist [I have since been here on a fresh sunny morning and it was breath-taking in its perfection]. On the way up I passed Milecastle 40, outlined in the grass. Then came several more gaps, in one of which the Wall again requires its ditch. On one of the intervening summits the familiar form of a turret, No 40B, brought a homely touch into the misty desolation. Farther on, a green platform marked the site of Milecastle 41 (Melkridge). Between this and the next milecastle (Cawfields) are several gaps, in some of which the ditch is again found, in one case for only a few yards, a memorial to Roman thoroughness. Cawfields milecastle is in fine condition, its walls eight feet thick and rising to eight courses: the sloping ground shows up its south gate well and the bolt hole for securing the doors can be seen. Here was found a tombstone to a Pannonian soldier erected by Pusinna, presumably his wife.

A little farther on we descend to Cawfields quarry, with a small lake in its excavation. To avoid this, which has destroyed the Wall and the ridge on which it stood, one must descend almost to the Vallum, now re-approaching the Wall. It is in fine condition here, without causeways, but accompanied by the 'marginal mound' composed of upcast from a later recutting and cleaning. The gaps in the original mounds are clear in the northern, but have not been completed in the southern, mound.

Beyond the quarry we come to a road running down from the Military Road and beyond this the Haltwhistle Burn comes swirling down in wide curves from Broomlee and Greenlee Loughs some miles to the north-east. Here can be seen the green ramparts of Haltwhistle Burn fort, only three-quarters of an acre in extent, built on the Stanegate shortly before the Wall and destroyed after the latter was erected. Around this are the outlines of several 'temporary camps' such as the legions threw up when halting for the night during an expedition, though it is thought that some at least may have housed the builders of the Wall. If, as seems likely, the legionaries met considerable opposition during the building, defensive precautions would be as necessary as when they were on the march. And in any case, the builders had to live somewhere during those busy years.

At the road and the burn the Wall makes a sharp turn to the right. Here I lost it for a while. Looking back, I could see the Vallum descending the hill behind the quarry, but beyond the road – nothing. Perhaps I was becoming wall-eyed: at any rate I crossed the burn by a small bridge and struck out in the direction indicated on the map, but after casting about for three-quarters of an hour I found myself back at my starting point, like Alice through the Looking Glass. Eventually I found it by following the road to the quarry and leaving this after it crossed the burn by another bridge. Turning left by a cottage, where the wall ditch runs on the right, and proceeding upwards, I suddenly found myself at Greatchesters. The mist had developed into a drizzle, then into a steady downpour, and I had been ploughing through long wet grass, against which there is no protection short of gum-boots: also I had to get back to the 'Bognor' for the night and every step onwards meant another back later on. I had reached another fort and might as well halt there and examine it on the morrow, perhaps in better weather. So I tramped back the three long dreary miles of the Military Road, feeling like a drowned rat but cheered by the prospect of a bath and another of Mrs Ridley's 'plain teas'. *O si sic omnes* who purport to produce meals of that name.

I had reason to be grateful that the rain had shortened my day, for at tea I found that Dr Smith had a visitor, none other than Professor Richmond himself, on his way to inspect excavations at Bewcastle. I felt much as a biographer might on being unexpectedly confronted with the subject of his biography in the flesh, or like a poacher caught by the gamekeeper, for here was the greatest living authority on Hadrian's Wall. After tea I was introduced and took the opportunity to put what I hope were intelligent questions on the many problems surrounding the Wall and the Romans in Britain. I certainly learnt a great deal in the three-quarters of an hour which Professor Richmond was kind enough to spare me. Among other things, he stressed that the seeming confusion in the original plans for the Wall sprang less from Roman incompetence than from their deliberate adoption of a process of trial and error. I was interested, too, to hear his views on the campaigns of Severus and the problems surrounding the 'departure of the Romans'. On the former, I gathered that he did not look kindly on recently-aired suggestions for postponing the division of the British province into two till after that emperor's death, and for assigning to him a reoccupation of the Antonine Wall. We had a most interesting discussion on the end of Roman Britain, but here Professor Richmond emphasized the need for much further excavation before the problem can be solved. Above all, I was impressed by his infectious enthusiasm for the Wall and all that appertains to its history. It is always a delight to meet a great scholar, not only for the learning one encounters, but for the courtesy which they (unlike some lesser lights) always extend to anyone interested in their subject. Here was I, an unknown intruder on a great man's special domain, yet I was treated as if I were a fellow *savant*.

Outside, the rain continued relentlessly and we were glad of a fire, for it was miserably cold. Yet this was the longest day of 1954!

10

GREATCHESTERS TO GILSLAND

There is still sun on the wall.
Proverbs of Sancho Panza

To my surprise, Tuesday dawned brilliantly after the previous evening's rain. From my room I could see the broad breast of the hill climbing to Winshields, whose outline stood out vividly against a deep blue sky. In the garden rhododendrons and lupins were almost vocal in their freshness. But my shoes were still so wet that I had to improvise insoles with sheets of newspaper. Mrs Ridley thought it was too fine to last, but I tore myself from her hospitality, obtained a lift from a passing motorist and was soon at Greatchesters again.

This fort is almost six miles from Housesteads and contained three acres. Its Roman name was Aesica and it was garrisoned successively by the Sixth Cohort of Nervians from Gaul, the Sixth of Raetians, from the district of the upper Danube, and the First or Second of Asturians. It occupies a delightful position. The ground slopes down to the south, where is a line of slender trees, with a ridge beyond and in the distance the blue outline of mountains: to the north is a lonely ridge crowned with larches: while eastwards one has a magnificent view back to Winshields. There is not so much to see as at Housesteads and Chesters, and in fact the whole area has not yet been excavated: most of the digging was undertaken as long ago as the Nineties. But the ramparts and their surrounding ditch show up well: on the west there are no fewer than four ditches, all clearly defined. It will be noticed that, like

Housesteads, the fort does not project beyond the Wall and that it faces east, for the same reason, the slope of the ground to the south. There are four gates, the Military Way entering by the eastern and leaving by the western. The west gate is the only one now left in any Wall fort so as to show the original work and the successive blockings until it was completely closed. In the east tower of the south gate stands an altar on which a libation cup is sculptured and in its west tower was found a hoard of jewellery, probably lost in the disaster of 197 and including the famous Aesica brooch, mentioned above.

In 1939 the foundations of Milecastle 43 and of the broad Wall to which it was attached were discovered under the narrow Wall which forms the side of the fort. The narrow Wall to the west of the fort was found to stride over the northern end of the four western ditches. So the ditches of the fort had been dug long before the change from broad to narrow Wall was decided upon. At least two ditches have recently been found on the eastern side and it is thought by some that this fort was originally planned as a large one, but that this plan was abandoned in favour of a later small fort, built when it was decided to add a fort at Carrawburgh.

Inside the fort can be seen the remains of the strong room under the 'chapel', with a complete arch over its entrance, all within railings. South-west of this are six rooms of a barrack-block. An inscription of 225, under Alexander Severus, found in the fort, records the rebuilding from the ground of a granary which had collapsed through age – not, be it noted, by enemy action, a useful reminder of the long periods of tranquillity which reigned in Roman Britain, even on its frontiers. We have to realize that from the Claudian conquest to the generally-accepted date of the 'departure of the legions' spans 364 years, the same period as separates us from the last decade of Elizabeth I. In that time ten or twelve generations grew up who knew no other ruler than imperial Rome and who regarded themselves, not as Britons, but as Romans, though Romans in a quite different sense from those of republican days.

An altar to Fortune was erected by a detachment of the Raetian spearmen, irregular troops armed with a throwing-spear called a 'gaesum'. Another was set up by a lady named Romana to the *Di Veteres*, who must be the Celtic god Hueter, here latinized into 'the old gods'. One wonders exactly whom this Romana thought she was honouring. These monuments are now at Newcastle, together with a mill-stone from here, inscribed 'Century of Antoninus, Mill number seven'. From here, too, came a tombstone to an adjutant (*cornicularius*) set up by his sister, which suggests that he was a Briton, recruited into the foreign garrison, for otherwise his sister would hardly have been here.

A hundred yards south of the fort stood the bath-house, the outlines of which showed up under a crop of hay. Perhaps the most notable feature at Greatchesters was the aqueduct by which water was brought to the fort from the Caw Burn, as the upper course of Haltwhistle Burn is called. To tap this at a higher level than the fort the Roman engineers had to start at Saughy Brigg Washpool, almost a mile due north of Winshields, and to keep it from falling below the fort's level they had to carry the water by a 'leet' round the edges of hills by a most circuitous route of six miles. Professor Richmond calls this leet 'one of the most remarkable and best-preserved of military aqueducts in Britain'. It certainly was a considerable feat, and another testimony to the periods of security on the Wall, for its whole course lies north of that structure.

South of the fort was the *vicus* and beyond this the cemetery. Here was found a very roughly executed tombstone, now at Newcastle, 'To the memory of my daughter Pervica', with a figure of a child standing in a niche, a pathetic reminder of the *lacrimae rerum* which here, as elsewhere, left their mark on humble and exalted alike.

I left Greatchesters in grand weather and walked gently upwards to a farmhouse, beyond which was a small plantation of larches. This would be a perfect place for a picnic, with the sweet smell of the larches mingling with the persistent murmurings of wood pigeons, but I could not linger. To the north a solitary farmer was trenching his land, otherwise not a soul was in sight. To the south the Vallum showed up clearly, the crossings in its ditch and the gaps in its mounds being very distinct. I was now approaching Cockmount Hill, between which and Greatchesters the narrow Wall runs a little behind, instead of upon, the broad foundation, presumably because the second set of engineers distrusted the work of their opposite numbers earlier. Here one comes to the 'Nine Nicks of Thirlwall', so called because the ridge on which the Wall runs is broken into successive peaks separated by depressions, repeating on a smaller scale the features of the more rugged section from Sewingshields to Cawfields. This is another delightful part of the walk, with pleasant views as one climbs and descends many times but without great effort. The ditch re-appears in the gaps and the Wall dutifully makes its usual re-entrants. Actually there are now only seven 'nicks', two having been destroyed by quarrying. One would have thought that in this lonely area the pleasing works of Nature would have been safe from industrial inroads, especially where they carried such a monument as the Roman Wall, but nothing is sacred where profits or planners are concerned. And, after all, buildings and roads must continue to be made and the materials must come from somewhere, that is, from the English countryside. We are gradually reducing England to a well-planned dull flatness, unconsciously fulfilling the prophecy 'Every valley shall be exalted and every mountain shall be made low' – one of the two biblical texts to which I have always taken exception (the other being the apocalyptic promise that there shall be no more sea). That British Solomon, James I, prophesied that in time 'England will be all London', and though he was a little premature we have since gone a long way to fulfil his grim prophecy. Our coasts are gradually becoming one long promenade, complete with shelters and deckchairs; each city, town and village puts out suburban tentacles; and satellite and 'overspill' towns, designed by planners to cure the evil, only intensify it. National parks are established by one authority and immediately claimed by another for hydro-electric development. One department urges us to grow more food, while others seize good farming land for aerodromes, camps and open-cast mining. When will it be realized that there is only a certain amount of dry land in England and that each inroad destroys something priceless for ever, or at least for centuries?

I passed a turret on the way up, then the ruins of Milecastle 44, and then climbed to Muckleback Crag, 860 feet, the highest of the 'nicks'. At the west end of the summit Turret 44B is ensconced in a bend of the Wall. It was full of nettles, but otherwise in good condition. Descending, one is in Walltown Gap, wider than the previous ones, enfiladed by the Wall, which is again supplemented by its ditch. Just behind is a spring once called 'King Arthur's Well', but now provided with a prosaic manhole-cover within a fence. To the south, a farmhouse nestles charmingly in the trees. It was at Walltown, but not in the present house, that lived John Ridley, brother of Bishop Nicholas Ridley, martyred under Mary Tudor, in 1555. The village has disappeared long since. William Hutton found only one house, with a Roman altar on each side of the front door, which the inhabitants used for washing their hands on.

Beyond the gap Hutton found the ascent 'so difficult that I sometimes was obliged to crawl on all fours'. I found it less arduous than that, but was glad to rest for a few minutes in Milecastle 45 on the summit. Between this and Turret 45A, which stands in good condition except for its front, the Wall is well preserved by the Ministry of Works. The morning sun had now given place to grey skies, but the rain held off. To the south-west there was mist over Cross Fell, but on the right the grey outline of the Cheviots showed up clearly.

From here the pilgrim is bereft of his Wall by the intrusion of a quarry, which cuts off about two hundred yards of it and eats into the cliff to the south. Beyond this is another stretch of Wall, with a turret in it, and then Greenhead Quarry, which has destroyed the last of the 'nicks'. I had to make a long détour southwards to a road which, after a wait for blasting operations, led me to Carvoran Farm and the site of the next fort. The farm lies just west of a crossroads running northwards from the Newcastle–Carlisle road. I inquired for the remains of the fort and was directed through the farmyard and along a wall westwards. Here I found the north-west angle of the fort, but there was little else to see. Turning right, that is, northwards, I soon recovered the Wall ditch running down the hill from the quarry to Thirlwall Castle. Halfway down the hill I found shelter from the wind behind a hedge a yard or two from the ditch and ate my lunch. The weather was now improving and *Sol invictus* obliged by a fitful appearance. I am sure that, had I lived under the pagan empire, and remained ignorant of Christianity, I should have been a staunch adherent of that genial deity.

Though there is not much to see at Carvoran, the fort has several interesting features. It lies, not on the Wall, but on the Stanegate, like Chesterholm, yet so near the Wall that it must be regarded as part of that complex structure. Its original purpose was to guard the junction of the Stanegate and the Maiden Way, a Roman road coming up northwards from Kirkby Thore, where it left the transverse road from Catterick to Carlisle. As such, it may have been first erected by Agricola, though no trace of a pre-Hadrianic fort has yet been found. It will be noticed that the Vallum deviates – to the north this time – as if to avoid a fort just to its south, though this deviation is generally explained by the presence of a bog. For this fort, exceptionally, lies south of both Wall and Vallum. It was one of the few wall forts built late in Hadrian's reign. An inscription recovered from here is dated 136–8. It is only three miles from Greatchesters and it would seem that, like Carrawburgh and possibly Greatchesters, it was added to strengthen the defences on a difficult section of the Wall.

The fort covers three and a half acres. Its name is given as Magnae in the *Notitia*, which shows its garrison as the Second Cohort of Dalmatians. These hardy troops, used to the bleak mountains of Jugoslavia, would be inured to the rains and snows of Northumberland, but one wonders whether those who came from the sunny coastlands did not sometimes pine for their warmer homeland, voicing those feelings long afterwards so movingly expressed by Matthew Arnold:

> Far, far from here,
> The Adriatic breaks in a warm bay
> Among the green Illyrian hills; and there
> The sunshine in the happy glens is fair,
> And by the sea and in the brakes,
> The grass is cool, the sea-side air
> Buoyant and fresh, the mountain flowers
> More virginal and sweet than ours.

In Hadrian's time the fort was occupied by the First Cohort of Hamian archers from Syria. This is the only detachment of archers known in Roman Britain, a reminder that the bow and arrow, so important in the Middle Ages, were only subsidiary arms under the Romans, though mounted archers were not uncommon in the later Empire.

The fort, and the neighbouring *vicus*, have yielded many interesting inscriptions. There was an altar to the Imperial Fortune, for the well-being of Hadrian's adopted son, who died just before him, erected by the prefect of the Syrian archers 'because of a vision', a poem in honour of Julia Domna, the Syrian wife of Septimius Severus, apostrophized under the guise of Virgo of the Zodiac, here equated with Ceres and a Syrian goddess; and a tombstone set up by a legionary soldier to his blessed wife (*coniugi sanctis-*

simae) Aurelia Itala of Salona in Dalmatia, who lived thirty-three years without blemish (*sine ulla macula*). Presumably this soldier had been seconded for service with the auxiliaries, for if he had been employed in building the Wall he would hardly have had his wife with him. Then there was an altar to the nymphs (unspecified, but probably those presiding over the neighbouring Tipalt Burn, which surely deserves such guardians) erected by a lady and her daughter, presumably the wife and child of an officer in the garrison. Another was dedicated to Epona, patron goddess of horses. Readers of the *Golden Ass* will remember how Lucius, translated into an ass like Bully Bottom, was promised restoration to his human form on eating rose-petals, and how he tried in vain to reach the garland of roses round an image of Epona set up in a stable.

Little excavation has been done at Carvoran. Reginald Bainbrigg, headmaster of Appleby Grammar School, who supplied Camden with much information about these parts and himself walked large sections of the Wall, described the fort as 'a huge ruinous building builded four square ... from thence goeth a street called Mayden Way, which is paved with stones throughout the moors, about some forty miles in length, to Mayden Castle upon Stainemoor. The Picts' Wall a little above Caruoran upon very high strong rocks stands xi foot high and about ix foot broad.' It is sad to think that it has shrunk to its present exiguous remains with no one to stop this destruction. A sketch made in 1832 when the altar first mentioned above was found shows it standing amidst buildings four courses high. Even in 1859 an excursion organized by the Newcastle Society of Antiquaries found the bases of several columns, of which sections were lying around, and a sphinx-like figure and a terra-cotta head.

On the Wall, just west of where the Vallum resumes its course after its northward deviation, is the site of Milecastle 46, obviously built before a fort was thought of here. Continuing down the descending ditch of the Wall, I soon came, through a small wood, to a farmhouse in the valley, with external steps up to a loft. I was obviously trespassing, but was welcomed and taken along a passage which went right through the house, to be shown an inscribed stone built into its wall, upside down, recording the erection of or repairs to part of the Wall by the *Civitas Dumnoniorum*, the tribe occupying the Devonian peninsula. It will be appreciated that the Romans preserved most of the tribal units they found in Britain, suppressing their warring independence, but allowing them considerable self-government, operated from the chief urban centre of each. Similar records of the work of units from Hertfordshire and Dorset have been found. It is thought that these may represent forced labour requisitions by the government to assist the legionaries or more probably to carry out repairs at a later date.

Perched on a hill above the farm stands Thirlwall Castle, with a lofty ruinous fourteenth-century tower on which, I was told, a flag was planted at great hazard by an intrepid youngster to celebrate the coronation of the Queen the previous year. I had great difficulty in understanding my willing informant's northern speech, and as I left a sheep-dog, who had eyed me with suspicion from the first, gave me a sharp nip in the calf – the only 'unkind cut' I experienced in the whole of my tour. Here I left the Wall in search of a drink, striking left to the railway line and then to the inn at Greenhead along the banks of the Tipalt Burn. This is a delightful little stream, running down from the northern moors but here flowing placidly to join the South Tyne, its banks fresh with marvellous flowers, while ducks carried on their business on its shallow waters.

The sun was now out in genial earnest, and after a short rest I climbed the hill beyond the railway to see the large 'temporary camp' at its top. From there I had a good view of the pleasant country around – the wooded Tipalt valley immediately below and gentle hills beyond. We have now left the grandest parts of the Wall country and are in an entirely new milieu. There are no more beetling crags and

wide lonely moors, and the country is more like that of the
south, unpretentious but smiling, and full of farms and
villages. We are only a few hundred feet above sea level.
Unfortunately, this means that the tillers of the soil have
been at work for centuries, wresting a living from the land
and oblivious of the living history around them. So we shall
see fewer remains of the Wall and its attendant structures
from here onwards. But its ditch and the Vallum, which I
now rejoined, are still well marked: the former is twenty
feet deep in places. The Vallum hereabouts has been only
partially defaced by the Romans, the gaps having been
made in its mounds but no causeways, as at some places
farther east. It was slow going here, as the works run
through numerous farms and I progressed by continual
deviations to north and south. I passed Turret 47B on the
road from the station and so came to Gilsland.

Gilsland is a pleasant little town, situated on the Irthing, a
tributary of the Eden and quite a sizeable stream here. Unlike any other place we have touched, the town has preten-
sions as a holiday centre and points to several convales-
cent homes on its outskirts as evidence of its bracing air.
Just west of the station the Poltross Burn flows through a
deep wooded gorge into the Irthing from the south and
forms the boundary between Northumberland and Cumberland. It was barely four o'clock and I seemed to have
covered very few miles this day. But there had been a lot to
see on the way and I had to consider a refuge for the night,
which I knew I should not find farther west for many miles.
I therefore decided to put up at Gilsland and spend the rest
of the day exploring its surroundings. I made for the
vicarage, in the grounds of which I had read a fine stretch
of the Wall is preserved under the care of the Ministry of
Works. I found that it is now the 'Roman Way' Guest
House and my heart rose at the prospect of actually sleep-
ing on the Wall, as it were, under the combined aegis of
IOM and MOW. But my hopes were dashed: all rooms
were taken, and the same reply met my inquiry at a Guest

House opposite. Finally I found a room in the town and after a bath and tea sauntered out in delightful warm sun to see what I could see.

First I went up the road beyond the station, hoping to have a good view of the Vallum hereabouts, but though I went on and on for half a mile I could find no trace of it. I was rewarded, however, by a magnificent prospect to the north over Thirlwall Common, really a moor, with distant hills beyond and a splendid sky above. Returning to the station, I was met by an old goose with a band of goslings, protesting raucously with outstretched neck at my intrusion. I suppose there are few more ridiculous sights, unless it be a politician ranting about his 'standard of living'. Not that I despise politicians *en bloc*, and I do not include statesmen in that category. No one who has studied Roman history can fail to regret that the Empire did not develop, instead of stifling, political liberty: and if we are to have liberty we must tolerate considerable folly in order that truth and wisdom shall make themselves heard. But we have fools in plenty, doping the people with slogans and never more ridiculous than when they pontificate. Gibbon pointed the danger here when he remarked that 'Augustus was sensible that mankind is governed by names; nor was he deceived in his expectation, that the senate and people would submit to slavery, provided they were respectfully assured that they still enjoyed their ancient freedom.' Now, as then, the greatest threat to freedom comes from the state, whether controlled by a single autocrat, by privileged groups (whether based on birth or economic power) or even by the sovereign people. All these will abuse whatever power they can acquire, and the surest bulwark of freedom is not so much the rule of the majority as the limitation of the sphere of government – of the matters which the state, even if it represents the majority, may control.

But to return to our Wall. Going under the station subway and turning sharp right, I followed its course to the Poltross Burn, which I crossed by a wooden bridge, and at

the top of the steps found Milecastle 48, hemmed in by the
railway and not in very good shape. Several courses of wall
can be seen under the railway embankment. This was excavated in 1909 and found to be seventy by sixty feet internally. A flight of steps allowed the height of the wall on its
ramparts to be calculated at twelve feet, to which should be
added a parapet. In the north-west corner were found ovens
for cooking by a fire which was withdrawn when the
interior was hot and the food inserted in its place. It seems
a tricky process, but I am assured that the culinary result is
excellent.

From here the Wall runs down and then up through the
grounds of Roman Way Guest House, as mentioned above.
The proprietress willingly allowed me to inspect this and it
is well worth seeing, for it shows better than elsewhere the
narrow Wall standing on the broad foundation. In the
garden are several Roman altars and stones, but many that
were here have now, I was told, been removed to Corbridge. Two of the altars found here had formerly for centuries served as altar steps to Over (or Upper) Denton
Church.

After supper I made a short excursion to this little Norman church, a couple of miles south-west of Gilsland. The
first church was built by the Romans, who made the
chancel arch from one of the Roman gateways of Birdoswald fort. It holds only fifty and has no vestry. Near by is
a roofless Pele Tower and in the churchyard is the grave of
Margaret Teasdale, the Meg Merrilees of Scott's *Guy Man-
nering*. Her tombstone is inscribed:

> Here lieth the Body
> of Margaret
> Teasdale of Mumps
> hall who Died May
> the 5th 1777 aged 98
> years

What I was once some may relate,
What I am now is each one's fate,
What I shall be some may explain,
Till he that called Call again.

Keats has a poem about her, but hardly in his best vein. Next to her lies Margaret Carrick, who died in 1717 in her hundredth year.

As I returned to Gilsland came the first rain of the day, a disappointment after the delightful afternoon. But it was soon over and I could not grumble in that year of rare sunshine.

Sestertius of Caracalla, commemorating victory in Britain

11

GILSLAND TO CASTLESTEADS

That wall is so *very* narrow.
LEWIS CARROLL, *Through the Looking Glass*, ch. vi

Wednesday, June 23rd, opened with rough weather after rain during the night. Bursts of sun alternated with threatening overcast, and big black and white clouds piled up in startling contrast. There was half a gale of wind and it was much cooler. But it was good weather for walking, apart from the wind, which local prophets said would at least keep the rain off. And so I left Northumberland and took my first steps in a new county.

I picked up the Wall opposite Roman Way Guest House, where its course follows a pleasant lane westwards. Immediately to our right another fine stretch of Wall is preserved by the Ministry, eleven courses high and containing Turret 48A, flanked for a few feet on each side by the broad Wall. The lane continues prettily in the ditch of the Wall itself and presently Turret 48B is seen on the left. It is not so well preserved, only eighteen courses high, and when I passed was occupied by an incongruous hen-coop. At the farm here one must pay a small fee to continue down to the Irthing.

This river, if not quite so broad as the Tyne at Chesters, presented an equally formidable problem to the Roman engineers, especially as its west bank rises almost vertically to a height of fifty or seventy feet. The lane makes a wide sweep down to the flat eastern bank, where considerable remains of the abutment of the Roman bridge are preserved. There was more to be seen in Camden's day, for he wrote: 'The Picts' Wall passed the river Irthing by an arched bridge at a place called Willowford.' It is curious that Camden describes both bridges, here and at Chesters, as arched, whereas the last one at Chesters, at least, was of wood, as was probably that at Willowford also. It is a pity he did not give more details of the remains he saw, to justify his description.

The Wall can be traced as a grassy bank descending the hill: then we find four courses of the broad foundation, carrying the narrow Wall, and presently the foundations of a large tower behind the Wall. Beyond this was a turret, only a corner of which, recessed into the Wall, now remains, and beyond that an abutment running diagonally back from the Wall. North of the Wall the berm between it and the ditch was protected on the river bank by a large stone embankment. These works were built for the first bridge, the width of the Wall and therefore for foot-traffic only, but later they were considerably extended. The Wall was carried across the first abutment to end in two narrow culverts, which are thought to have been mill-races. Later still the splayed abutment south of the Wall was extended westwards, blocking the eastern culvert, and a pier, as wide as this new abutment – thirty-four feet – was built a few feet beyond it. The bridge had clearly been widened to its south to take wheeled traffic. Square grooves for its timber supports can be seen in the stones. The water-space between pier and abutment probably housed a water mill, for it was paved and a spindle-bearing from here lies at the corner of the tower. Thus the Romans, as at Chesters, had turned the obstacle of the river into a welcome source of power. The abutment, it will be noticed, ends some thirty yards east of the river, which has clearly, like the North Tyne at Chesters, changed its course during the intervening centuries. Possibly, therefore, the cliff beyond was not then so steep: otherwise it is hard to see how even the Romans ran their Wall up it.

Unfortunately, the cliff is steep now, and what is more,

there is no longer any bridge. So, discarding shoes and socks, and rolling up my trousers, I waded over the river. It was easy enough, though the dark swirling waters rose well above my knees, except for the thought that one false step amidst the invisible slippery rocks in the river-bed would earn me, and my pack, a disastrous ducking. Then, like a cat-burglar, or a monkey, I pulled myself up the muddy cliffs with the aid of convenient, or in spite of inconvenient, branches, and found myself at Milecastle 49. This is sited on a fine open plateau, called Harrow's Scar, just behind the wooded cliff, with grand views back over the winding Irthing in its pleasant valley, where the wind swept the hay-fields in ever-shifting tones of shot green. Beyond, the Nicks of Thirlwall reared their grassy crests, topped by fantastic ranks of gleaming cumulus clouds. In the milecastle, which measures seventy-five by sixty-five feet, a Ministry of Works attendant was happily mowing the grass with a scythe and volunteered the opinion that there would be no rain so long as the wind kept up. Thus cheered on my way and glad to be on level ground again, I soon found myself at the bottom of Birdoswald.

This fort is approached from the road which has joined the Wall from the north just before. Its north-western corner is occupied by a farmhouse, which exacts a small charge for admission. The site is inspiring – a plateau protected by a slight valley to the north and ending south-wards in a grassy projection beyond which cliffs fall steeply away to the wooded valley of the Irthing, seen winding in many a silvery bend far below, with delightful rolling country stretching for miles beyond to the misty fells. I longed to linger on the point of this projection and drink in the whole marvellous scene, but time forbade, and in any case the wind was too strong for peaceful contemplation. So I addressed myself to an understanding of this complicated structure.

The fort is only three and a quarter miles from Carvoran and enclosed five and a third acres. Its name was Camboglanna, meaning crooked bank or glen. If Mr O. G. S. Crawford's surmise is correct, that this name is the equivalent of Camlann, the last of King Arthur's twelve battles as given in the *Historia Brittorum*, where that hero received his death-wound, then Birdoswald is one of the most romantic spots in Britain. The *Notitia* garrisons it with the First Aelian Cohort of Dacians, from what is now eastern Hungary and Roumania, whose native weapon, a curved sword, is seen on a stone, now at Newcastle, commemorating the rebuilding of the west gateway about 217–19. Several other inscriptions, now at Carlisle, attest their presence here: one is surmounted by a swastika between two wheels containing crosses, looking for all the world like hot cross buns. Earlier the First Cohort of Tungrians, afterwards at Housesteads, may have been here.

I have mentioned earlier that in Cumberland the Wall was originally built of turf and only later replaced by stone. This change to turf, to be accurate, began at Willowford. It was the turf Wall, therefore, with its ditch in front, on which Birdoswald fort was built. Like many of the eastern forts, its *praetentura* projected beyond the Wall, which joined it at its main east and west gates. As the Wall was built first, the north portals of these gates had to cross the Wall ditch by a special foundation. But when, very soon afterwards in this sector, the turf Wall was replaced, the new stone Wall was brought up to the north wall of the fort. Recently the foundations of Turret 49A TW ('Turf Wall') were discovered in the centre of the section of turf Wall running across the fort, showing that this fort, like its fellows, was an afterthought. The Vallum bends to the south to avoid the fort, but as the latter was so near the cliff there was no room for its northern mound. Its ditch was crossed by a stone-revetted causeway, as at Benwell. The Vallum was defaced soon after construction, and a ditch outside and parallel to the walls of the fort was started but never finished. On the projecting plateau south of the fort signs of an earlier native promontory fort were found, which was itself replaced by a small Roman station apparently built before the Wall was contemplated. At the bottom of a ditch here were found numerous fragments of Roman tents, made as usual of leather and now on view at Tullie House, Carlisle.

We may now inspect the remains of the fort still visible, remembering that unfortunately this will be our last opportunity. It is sad to reflect that, of the sixteen forts on the Wall itself, only Chesters, Carrawburgh, Housesteads, Greatchesters, Carvoran and Birdoswald have anything to show us above ground and *in situ*. I entered the fort by its east gate, which is of the usual double type and in fine condition, though the later blockings were removed by the nineteenth-century excavators. The sockets in the pivot-stones of the portals are clear. The north portal when blocked became a guard-room and the original guard-room on its north side was turned into a tile-kiln and was later restored with a platform which may, it is thought, have mounted a catapult or *ballista*. The reader may remember that a similar operation at Housesteads converted a guard-room into a coal-store. A pillar is still standing here eight feet high: two arches lie dismantled on the ground: a reconstruction of the south guard-room furnished it with a hypocaust. Just north of this gate is an interval tower, excavated as recently as 1951 and twelve courses high.

Halfway between the east gate and the south-east corner was a postern gate, not now visible, but matched by another on the west wall. For this fort, like Benwell, Rudchester and Chesters, had six gates, one double one on each side and an extra single one on each of its longer sides. The south-east corner tower is well-marked, also the rounded corner of the fort, like that of a playing-card. Faint traces of the Vallum ditch can be seen just beyond. The south gate is not in so good condition as its eastern fellow. The south-west corner is little more than a mound, but the postern in the west wall is exposed, with wheel-ruts on its threshold and pivot-blocks for its doors. The main west gate is covered by a shrubbery, but in the lane forming the side entrance to the farm can be seen the north-west curve of the fort wall, still standing twelve courses high. From this angle the Wall itself went off westwards, but was demolished when the modern gateway was made.

The interior of the fort has been partly excavated, but most of the finds have been covered up. Photographs of some of these can be seen at Tullie House, showing four successive building periods. There were the usual headquarters, commandant's house, barracks and granaries. A building-stone recorded the construction of a portion of the Wall by the British fleet, instead of legionaries as usual. Two inscriptions showed for the first time that Hadrian's Wall escaped the disaster under Commodus which overwhelmed that of Antonine and that its first destruction occurred when Clodius Albinus took the British forces to Gaul in his bid for empire. One records the restoration of the commandant's house by the Dacian cohort and a *numerus* under Severus: the other that of a granary by the Dacians and the First Cohort of Thracians in the same reign. Yet another slab commemorates the rebuilding of the headquarters, commandant's house and baths under Diocletian and his three colleagues just after the second destruction in 296. It states that the commandant's house had fallen in ruins and was covered with earth – a testimony to the fierceness of the barbarian fury. Professor Richmond regards this as an admission of neglect also, but must we not allow Constantius time to restore Roman rule in Britain as a whole and to repair destruction at York and other places farther south? At Birdoswald the Constantian reconstruction was well planned but poorly executed, and that after the disaster of 367 was even poorer. Soon after 375 an unevacuated barrack was looted and burnt. Dr Kent claims that one of the coins found here, but now dispersed, was later than 383, the traditional date for the abandonment of the Wall.

From Birdoswald the Romans built a road running north-west in a straight line to the outpost fort of Bewcastle, climbing to 1000 feet over Gillalees Beacon, on the top of which a signal-station was erected. This fort – in which stand the church and castle, with the famous Saxon cross – was called Banna, meaning 'the peak', and covered six acres and housed a thousand men. It was built under Hadrian to act as a forward 'eye' to the Wall, which is here masked by high ground to its north. Its garrison was withdrawn by Theodosius after the great disaster of 367. Vivid evidence of its earlier destruction in 296 was found in its shrine. The underground strong room was choked with rubbish, wall plaster and burnt beams, which had fallen through the burnt floor of the shrine above. I had hoped to interrupt my mural walk by a visit to Bewcastle, but after negotiating the Irthing and inspecting Birdoswald the day was too far advanced for the twelve-mile détour.

From Birdoswald a very pleasant secondary road follows the course of the Wall westwards, but the latter is visible only here and there. I met practically no traffic here, save a large American car covered with baggage and carrying a man and a woman sitting at opposite ends of the wide front seat, as if they were contemplating mutual separation. Another such had decanted a party while I was at Birdoswald, to whom I tried to explain the lay-out of the fort with the aid of my plan, but they seemed only mildly interested and asked me whether I had seen the wall at Londonderry. No doubt the wind made antiquarian curiosity rather difficult.

The sector between Milecastles 49 and 51 is interesting in that there the stone Wall was not built on the line of its turf predecessor, but ran more or less parallel to the latter a little to the north. It is of course the narrow Wall, the broad foundation underlying the narrow Wall from near Brunton to Willowford only. It is the stone Wall that the road follows. Not far from Birdoswald, just after Turret 49B, I passed a good stretch of Wall on the left under the care of the Ministry, a gang of whose men were busily at work on it. I exchanged a few words with them, but had not time to watch just how they carried out their excellent work of restoration. I was told that they are careful to replace each stone in its original place: no fancy additions are allowed.

The turf Wall could be seen at places in the fields on the left, in one place showing up well under growing hay. Beyond, the Vallum is also clearly seen, running parallel. Excavations here showed that the stone Wall was built under Hadrian, thus putting out of court a theory once held that that Emperor's wall was wholly of turf and that its stone successor was the work of Severus. They also showed that the Vallum was later than the turf Wall, since it deviated to the south to avoid Milecastle 50 TW, but so closely that its north mound was omitted. Here was found a small part of a wooden tablet recording building by the Second Legion under Platorius Nepos in the time of Hadrian. This precious piece of wood was so small that it contained only part of a P, the upright of an L, and the tops of three preceding letters, with the bases of three more in the line above, yet the late Professor Collingwood was able to restore the whole inscription, containing fourteen words, with absolute certainty. To one accustomed to medieval and Tudor manuscripts, where similar destruction would have proved fatal, such a feat appears a piece of incredible wizardry. It was aided, of course, by the formal nature of the inscription, but even so is an outstanding performance. It is admirably reproduced, on a larger scale, at Tullie House. Some distance farther on one can turn down a lane to the left and see where a section has been cut through the turf Wall, revealing its alternating bright and dark structure resulting from the laying of turf upon turf.

To do justice to this sector I should have returned to Birdoswald along the turf Wall and thus examined both works in their whole length, but time forbade. I pressed on, and on reaching a turret realized to my horror that I had been day-dreaming and had forgotten to look at the indispensable Bruce-Richmond for a space. I had thus passed a lodge on the left of the road labelled 'Coombe Crag' without realizing its importance. Retracing my footsteps for half a mile, I inquired directions for the Roman quarry where some excavating legionaries had carved their names in the rock. I was told to continue down the lane from the lodge until I came to a large yew tree. So on I went and soon found myself in breast-high bracken and surrounded by hundreds of trees, but not a single yew could I see. There was nothing to do but to return and try again. By great good luck I eventually succeeded. Go down the lane from the lodge, avoiding a cart track slightly to the left, and keep straight on by a narrow path which later veers left, descends slightly and crosses a small stream and then climbs to the rocks. On these are many modern hieroglyphs, but pass these and just as the path goes downwards the Roman inscriptions will be seen on the rock-face to one's right. Three names can be seen, MATERNVS (the M joined to the A and the E represented by II, as in Roman cursive writing), SECVRVS and IVSTVS. Somehow, these casual scribblings by unknown private soldiers, preserved in this lonely spot for so many centuries, gave me a greater thrill than many more pretentious monuments. I could have wished for Faustus' power to call up their spirits for an informal chat, to find out what part of the far-flung Empire they came from, what they thought of north Britain and where they ended their days. It is curious to reflect that of the thousands of troops who garrisoned the Wall for nearly three centuries we know even the names of only a few hundreds.

Talking of Faustus, lower down this cliff is an inscription mentioning Faustus and Rufinus, consuls in 210, which the experts declare is a forgery, apparently perpetrated by some scholar to prove that Severus built the Wall. Here is another psychological puzzle, that intelligent persons should go to such lengths to defend a theory which they must know in their hearts their forgery itself condemns, even if it is never exposed. One thinks inevitably of the

Piltdown mystery. I have just been reading letters in a Sunday paper arguing that the Princes in the Tower were murdered by Henry VII and not by Richard III, resuscitating old arguments that have long since been demolished by impartial historians. Then there are the cranks who try to prove that Shakespeare's plays were written by Bacon, or the Earl of Oxford, or some other. Surely the historian's duty is to search for truth, wherever it leads, and not to torture the evidence to prove a preconceived theory at all costs. This last is the greatest of sins, for it poisons the wells of truth and lies at the base of all the atrocities which have been committed in the name of ideologies in recent years. And false history, once established, takes an unconscionable time to eradicate. The legend of the Puritans, first started by the Whig historians, is still not quite dead in this country: one-sided views of the American Revolution helped to give post-war American policy an anti-British trend in certain respects, from which we are still suffering: and Russian distortions of history are food for Communist propaganda every day.

I took a quick lunch in a sheltered spot amidst the trees and then continued along the road. Here on the left the Vallum was particularly clear and this is the only place where it can be seen in its original state: for some reason it never suffered later defacement, partial or otherwise, on this stretch. Two turrets, 51A and B, sat unobtrusively on the right of the road. Then I passed Bankshead Farm, where Milecastle 52 was excavated in 1934 and found to be one of the largest of the whole series, ninety by seventy-seven feet internally. A little farther on the road descends to the Banks Burn, but at the top of the ridge, called Pike Hill, was a signal station twenty feet square. It was clearly intended to supplement the normal signal system of turrets and milecastles, and was sited diagonally on the Wall, which joined its south-east side from the east and left from its north-west side. From here is a wide view over northern Cumberland and messages could easily be sent to and received from Gillalees tower to the north. South-east of here, just across the Irthing, was Nether Denton, one of the forts on the Stanegate, but only occupied from Agricola's time till the Wall was built, if as long.

A little beyond Pike Hill, Turret 52A is seen on the left of the road some fourteen courses high, with about eighty yards of the stone Wall. At the bottom of the hill one must fork right and cross the burn, then climb Hare Hill opposite. Here is the highest fragment of the Wall now standing, two inches short of ten feet high, though only the core is original. Hutton 'viewed this relic with admiration', but I nearly missed it. It is on the right of the lane up the hill, almost opposite a white house called 'The Cottage' and a little below the farmhouse at the top. I owed my discovery to the farmer's wife, who gave me directions despite her preoccupation with a batch of appetizing tarts in her kitchen, having failed to get any reply to my knock at 'The Cottage'. In the north face of this fine piece of wall is a centurial stone, brought from a field near by, inscribed <PP, denoting the *primus pilus*, or senior centurion of a cohort, whose century built a sector here. It is the first stone from the left, about four feet up.

From the farm I continued westwards along a pleasant grass path. This part of my walk was easy from the walker's point of view, but tricky for the antiquary. For almost the first time I had neither road nor the continuous stone structure of the Wall to guide me and must trust to tracing the Wall by grassy mounds, easily confused with hedgerows, or by its ditch. In most cases it was the ditch which gave me the clearest clue, though I presently found that the path had been made by previous pilgrims and could be picked out ahead by white ladder-stiles over successive hedges. This is delightful rolling upland country, charmingly intimate, with its small farms scattered amidst fields brilliant with buttercups and sorrel, yet beyond I could see the distant outline of Cold Fell and farther still the heights of Criffell in Scotland, thirty-five miles away.

Just beyond the farm the Wall ditch was full of water, farther on it was covered with wild flowers. We now cross the Red Rock Fault, the dividing line between the limestone to the east and the red sandstone of Cumberland. It was of course this lack of limestone beyond this point which accounted for the Turf Wall in the original plan.

I now came to a coppice, through which runs the Burtholme Beck. Ascending beyond this, I found a stretch of Wall about seven feet high and surmounted by bushes: only its core remains, the facing stones having been completely robbed. It should be borne in mind that the Wall from Banks to its end at Bowness is no longer built to the narrow, but to what is called the intermediate, gauge. The Turf Wall, starting at the Irthing, was replaced within a few years by the narrow Wall as far as the Banks Burn, but west of that the replacing was carried out at leisure to a width of nine Roman feet. Just here the Wall area was unusually full of rabbits, which scattered in all directions as I approached. Beyond this piece of Wall the ditch swerves to the right for a stretch, the reason being that Turret 54A (Garthside) was here made of clay for lack of good turf and collapsed into the original ditch. A new turf wall was then built north of the old wall, with a new ditch beyond it, and a new turret placed behind the old one. This curious procedure suggests a lack of thoroughness on the part of the Roman engineers: rather than clear up the ruins they preferred to build round them. And as all this was done before the stone Wall was run up to the new turret, it was evidence for the delay in completing the stone structure throughout its length. Nor is this the whole story, for when the Wall was rebuilt after the disaster of 197 it was run across the ruins of the turret, which was no longer considered necessary.

On emerging from the valley formed by the burn I came to a cross-roads, beyond which I could see no trace for a time of either path or Wall. After several false starts, I found myself progressing precariously along the edge of a hayfield and at last emerged into a meadow, when I saw a curious object approaching with unsteady gait. I stood still and the creature, unsuspecting of my presence since he was to windward, revealed himself as a hedgehog heaving towards me as he slowly and carefully placed one foot before the other. Eventually he came within four inches of my toe before he halted and finally coiled himself into a prickly ball. These wanderings caused me to miss Howgill, where in a wall is a centurial stone commemorating work on the Wall by the *civitas catuvellaunorum*, the people around Verulam in Hertfordshire.

I now picked up the Wall again, descending towards the stream known as King Water, on its way to join the Irthing. Here I regained the road, which crosses the river and climbs parallel to and just south of the Wall up to the pleasant village of Walton. The ditch is plain to the right of the road, climbing towards the stocky church prominent on the summit. In the village, under which lies the foundation of Milecastle 56, I fell in with a man who showed me 'Roman Cottage', which he said was largely constructed of Roman stones from the Wall and presumably the milecastle. It was now nearly five and I inquired, none too hopefully, about the possibilities of tea. To my joy he thought his sister at the Black Bull might be able to help. I soon found myself in that commendable inn, seated comfortably in an ancient room with oak beams across its ceiling and a cavernous chimney, in which hams used to hang in earlier days. Here it was good to relax and to eat another marvellous 'plain tea', of which northerners alone seem to have discovered the secret and of which the high-spot in this case was a flat gooseberry tart made of the minutest berries I have ever seen in such quantity. Everyone has heard of the lunatic who beat his head with a hammer, because it was so pleasant when he left off: but a meal like this made up even for the lunacy of 'mural tourification'. Here I found a newspaper, the first I had seen since Sunday, and tried unsuccessfully to get abreast of the county cricket scores.

Through the window I looked out over a delightful garden resplendent with lupins and across the Irthing valley to the Tindale Fells, radiant in the mellow sunlight.

Then, through a landscape bathed in a golden sun, I tore myself from hospitable Walton and followed the path south-westwards. Old Hutton, by the way, found a bed here with much difficulty at the Cow and Boot Inn and nothing but milk to drink. But on his leaving in the morning, his land-lady would only take a few pence until he pressed two shillings on her.

There is little to guide one here, for the works have been fairly well effaced by centuries of tilling. The Black Bull stands roughly on the Wall itself: from there the path con-tinues beyond and almost at right angles to the north–south road, past some bungalows and then down to the Cam Beck. The Vallum, of which no sign appears, had increased its distance from the Wall as the latter climbed towards Walton: it then approached again, only to go off at an angle and to cross the beck considerably to the south. Here I struck the road running south to the west of the stream and, after failing to find any trace of Wall or ditch where they should have entered the grounds of Castlesteads, de-cided to postpone my visit to that fort till the morrow. I must now find accommodation for the night at Brampton, which meant a farther three miles' walk. Rather illogically, while taking every mile on the Wall in my stride, as part of my bargain, I somehow begrudged walking to and from it. But this time it was a joy merely to be in such delightful country on such a lovely evening. At Brampton I secured the last room at the Howard Arms, an old coaching inn full of interesting furniture, which was 'delicensed' by an ardent teetotal landlord, a former Countess of Carlisle. My room was a long attic, with sloping roof, containing three beds end to end, like ships of the line, and a minute window on the floor; but I was lucky to get even that, as motorists were coming here after being turned away from Carlisle.

After a welcome bath and supper, I walked leisurely out

to Old Brampton a mile west of the little town. Here, on a
steep red sandstone cliff overlooking the Irthing, was a
Roman fort, one of the series connected with the Stanegate,
which ran just to its north. That evening the site was ablaze
in the setting sun, whose light reddened even those red
cliffs. Old Brampton church, dedicated to St Martin, lies in
the fort's north-east angle: the cemetery to the west fills its
northern third. South of this traces of some of the central
buildings can be seen, as also the ramparts and ditch beyond the church. The dedication of the latter to St Martin
has been thought to indicate the activity in these parts of St
Ninian, the apostle of southern Scotland towards the end of
the fourth century. His chief foundation there, Candida
Casa (the white house) at Whithorn in Galloway, was likewise dedicated to St Martin, whom he is said to have previously met at Tours and whose example inspired his work.
If this is correct the late Roman *vicus* near here would have
been one of the first Christian communities near the Wall.
But Ninian's visit to Tours has been denied, and it is more
likely that both dedications date from later times, and so
throw no light on this problem.

Turning my back on the setting sun, I walked gently
back to Brampton. The wind had slackened, but was still
fresh, creating that fascinating pale-yellow light which gives
the north and west counties an ethereal beauty seldom
found in the more mellow south. Every tree and bush cast
the longest shadows and as I regained the town the sand-

Centurial stone from Carvoran

stone pile of the new church was aglow with flame. I had
walked about sixteen miles this day and, though there had
been nothing exciting to record, it had been one of my best.
I felt I had earned my rest and could count on a good day
tomorrow.

12

CASTLESTEADS TO CARLISLE

Ne sont que trois matières à nul home attendant,
De France et de Bretaigne et de Rome la grant.
                    JEAN BODEL, *Chanson de Saisnes*

Never were the omens for a fine day more meanly belied. It
was raining when I awoke and it continued without a pause
till late evening – *dies irae et vindictae, tenebrarum et
nebulae*. It seemed futile to follow the Wall in such a downpour, yet I must go on, whatever the weather. Like Macbeth, I had

> Stepp'd in so far, that should I wade no more,
> Returning were as tedious as go o'er.

Finally I compromised by deciding to spend the day in and
around Brampton and to return to my Wall next morning,
come what might. I could examine Castlesteads at leisure
and there was also another quarry near by with Roman
inscriptions.

As things turned out, I had quite a good morning. I took
a bus to where the little River Gelt passes under the Carlisle road on its way to join the Irthing. The reader who
desires to make this pleasant excursion should alight at a
white cottage on the left, with a large bungalow standing in
a fine garden on the opposite side, about two miles out of
Brampton. Here a side road branches eastward, following
the river upstream. Going up this, I inquired directions for
the 'written rock' at a cottage, where the road is replaced by
a path which crosses to the north bank of the Gelt, and was

told to follow this path for about half a mile, taking the lower of any forks so as to keep along the river's edge. This proved to be a delightful walk and I am surprised that this wooded gorge is not more widely known. It would be the ideal place in a heat wave, if such ever occur in these parts. One is completely shaded by trees, the path climbs and descends with irregular unexpectedness, and below, the river, whose name means 'wild man', boils impetuously over the iron-brown stones or simmers quietly in deep pools. There was no heat wave during my visit, but the trees effectually kept the rain out and the contrasting green and brown colouring filled the almost subterranean scene with unexpected light for such a gloomy day.

It was near here that the final battle in the Rising of the North against Elizabeth I was fought in February 1570. The previous November the Earls of Northumberland and Westmorland had raised the North on behalf of Mary Stuart and the old religion, but the captive Scottish Queen had been moved out of their reach and they had finally disbanded their troops and had fled to Scotland. Lord Leonard Dacre, a powerful local magnate with his seat at Naworth Castle, had not joined the rebels, but his actions had been equivocal and Elizabeth now ordered his arrest. This was easier said than done, for Dacre had several thousand loyal retainers at his call and Lord Hunsdon, at Berwick, could only scrape together 1500. With these he approached Naworth, a few miles east of where we now are, but found it strongly held: moving west, he was attacked by Dacre with a larger force. 'They gave the proudest charge that ever I saw,' wrote Hunsdon afterwards, knowing well his peril with the deep gorge of the Gelt behind him: but his arquebusiers stopped them and he then rode them down with his cavalry. That was the end of the rising, but had the day gone otherwise Elizabeth's throne might yet have been severely shaken. Hunsdon was rewarded by one of those epistles, in crabbed English, interlarded with Latin, and addressed by his Christian name, so

characteristic of the great Queen, in which the hint of
advancement made up for more tangible profit. After all, he
was her kinsman, and the régime which he had saved
existed as much for the advantage of him and the rest of the
ruling class as for her.

In due course I came to the footbridge and then, as in-
structed, returned for a few yards to some stone steps,
climbed a few of these and turned off on a path to the
right. Even then it was some time before I found the inscriptions and still longer before I clambered up, holding on
to branches, to read them. The main inscription records the
work of a unit (*vexillatio*) of the Second Legion under the
optio (centurion's deputy) Agricola in the consulship of
Aper and Maximus (207), but it is now sadly defaced. I
could only make out VEX.LLEG.II.AVG. and under that
SVB AGRICOLA O, with a few more indistinct letters to
the right. The inscription on the next rock had almost entirely flaked off. No doubt this quarry was working at high
pressure turning out stones for the rebuilding of the Wall
after the disaster of 197. It was the very next year that that
indefatigable emperor Septimius Severus arrived in person
to put things right.

Behind, the red rocks rise in huge vertical-sided blocks,
like some weird eastern city abandoned to the jungle. Half
a mile farther up the river some soldiers of the Sixth Legion
have written their names, but I despaired of finding these
without directions or some Ariadne's thread, which were
not forthcoming. Instead, I continued up the gorge and
came out by Talkin Tarn, a pretty piece of water the size of
the Round Pond, and my idea of what a round pond
should be. The meadows come down to the water without
bank or path and even on that grey day they contrived to
make a delightful contrast of green and blue.

So to lunch at Brampton. In the afternoon I walked out
to Castlesteads. The site of this fort lies in the grounds of
Castlesteads House, the entrance to which is on a by-road
turning off the Brampton–Longtown road just past the inn

beyond the Irthing Bridge. At the lodge I inquired of an old man working in his garden, but found that he was stone deaf, so I continued up the drive to a house on the left. Here I was told that the owner, Major-General G. F. Johnson, was absent and that it would be in order if I walked through, past the mansion house, to the summer-house, where there are several altars and inscribed stones.

The fort lies above the valley of the Cam Beck, which winds below to its north-west. Like Carvoran, it is not on the Wall, which crossed the beck farther north and then ran south-west on its opposite side. But unlike Carvoran it is enclosed by the Vallum, which deviates to the south to pass it, just north of Castlesteads House. It was nearly seven miles from Birdoswald and was comparatively small, covering only three and three-quarter acres. Its name was Uxellodunum, meaning high fort, and its garrison accord-ing to the *Notitia* the First Cohort of Spàniards. Earlier garrisons, according to inscriptions, included the Fourth Gauls, the First Batavians and possibly the Second Tun-grians. Unfortunately its site was buried when the gardens were laid out in 1791 and there is nothing now to be seen. Richard Bainbrigg reported in 1601 that a countryman building here 'sunk deep into the ruins of this castle, where he found fair and strong walls of hewen stone, among the which I saw the rarest work that ever I saw in my life: it was included after the manner of a quadrangle within four hewen walls, about some four ells broad: it stood upon many little arches which were black with fire: upon these arches stood a vault and upon that a fair level place finely plastered'. Clearly he had lighted upon a hypocaust. What a pity this wretched 'countryman' could not have quarried elsewhere for his stones or his eighteenth-century succes-sors have preserved what he did leave. The Age of Elegance was so fond of artificial ruins and 'Gothick' summer-houses, yet here was a unique ruin ready-made for them – and they just covered it up. They also demolished half a mile of Wall. These were the people who used Eltham Palace as a

barn and what is now Southwark Cathedral as a coal-shed:
while soon after Canterbury Castle was dismantled to make
a gas-works. The case of Newcastle Castle has already been
mentioned. We are wiser now, but the spirit of vandalism is
not quite dead. One remembers that in the last war some
English people clamoured for St Peter's to be bombed, not
only out of petty revenge, but to pamper their hatred of
'culture'.

To reach the summer-house one must go through an iron
gate into an enclosed garden and up the slope. In, or rather
just outside, it, though under cover, keeping company with
garden implements, are several interesting inscribed stones.
The finest is an altar erected to Jupiter, Best and Greatest,
by the second milliary cohort *equitata* of Tungrians, that is,
an infantry unit one thousand strong nominally, containing a
cavalry detachment. On one side is a thunderbolt and on
the other a wheel, both symbols of Jove – and found on
another altar from here now at Carlisle set up by the same
cohort under Gordian III in the third century. It is surmised that this cohort was not here in full strength, in view
of the smallness of the fort. Another large altar shows a
naked male figure with a hefty club in his right hand –
presumably Hercules. Another was dedicated to the Discipline of the Emperors, like that at Corbridge: it originally
read DISCIPLINAE AVGGG, indicating Severus and his
sons Caracalla and Geta, but after the death of the first-
named and the murder of the third two Gs were defaced
and VSTI engraved beneath. One would have thought that
this would have been a permanent memorial of the indis-
cipline of the surviving Emperor. Another stone has a single
long word, quite unlike any Roman inscription and apparently native: it is upside down, but even when reversed
has floored the experts. At Carlisle is another altar from
here to the Mothers of all peoples, the German triad mentioned earlier, recording the restoration by a senior centurion of a temple fallen into ruin by lapse of time, which,
as we have seen elsewhere, had ample opportunity to bring

slow destruction upon buildings and monuments, as well as the more dramatic ravages of war. From here, too, may have come an altar to Mithras which Camden recorded as at Naworth: if so, that god may have had a temple here besides the three farther east.

Returning to the lodge, I turned right, up the by-road which runs west of the fork, to pick up the Wall where it crosses the Cam Beck. It was wetter than ever and very muddy on the path by the stream, but I found the ditch of the Wall dug deep in the sandstone as it ran up the hill to a farmhouse which is built on the site of Milecastle 57. From there it is plain, climbing to the Longtown road, where I hoped to pick it up on the morrow. Here I met an old man carrying a bucket of oats to his hens, plodding along without coat in the downpour. I relieved him of his burden for a spell and he told me that he was eighty-four and came from Hawick over the Border. He pronounced this as one syllable, with a vowel-sound that I could never achieve if I tried all day.

So back to Brampton. My day of rest had taken me about eight miles. The rain had proved disastrous to others, causing the cancellation of the local school sports, for which I had seen youngsters hopefully preparing earlier. The school is a modern building in ordinary red brick, which clashes hopelessly with the paler sandstone of most of the town houses. The Romans were not the only builders who stuck to standard designs regardless of effect. Equally unhappy, to my mind, is the interior of Brampton Church, belying the promise of its fine external proportions and reddish stone. It is very dark inside and has been spoiled by lurid modern windows which I could only regard as disastrous.

Next morning the rain had mercifully stopped, but it was grey and cloudy and unseasonably chilly. After breakfast I set out for the Wall, but had to walk as far as the Irthing bridge before I obtained a lift up the hill. At the summit the Wall and ditch, coming up from the Cam Beck, continue along a road to the left. There was little to see and presently came a mist, which quickly developed into a downpour. Fortunately this did not last and I soon came to the remains of Milecastle 58. Where the road turns left to Irthington the Wall continues south-westwards along a footpath. Though the ground is only about one hundred and fifty feet above sea, one has a sense of height here as one looks westwards over the flats to Carlisle. There is a good stretch of the Wall here, topped with oaks, but thereafter it is difficult to follow. This was in fact the least pleasant part of my walk. There seemed to be neither Wall nor path and presently I found myself in a field of high wet grass, which drenched my shoes and grew just as high under the hedges where I tried to avoid it. I was tempted to revile the 'Wall, vile wall', excusing myself with the thought that even the enthusiastic Hutton was moved at times to call it 'that dreary wall'. My temper was not improved when, at last escaping from this interminable watery field, I caught myself in a regular booby-trap of barbed-wire fence and tore my raincoat. I now found myself in a sunk lane, once a drovers' road, indescribably muddy and filled with equally long and wet grass. That quotation from Macbeth, which I had thought so apposite, was having its revenge and I was literally 'wading through' this sector at least. But all lanes have an end and this one brought me at last to a farm, but unfortunately took a left turn and left me guessing. Finally I went through a gate, hoping to continue in the right direction across the field beyond, but had first to flounder through ankle-deep mud churned up by cattle. There followed more barbed-wire and more rents in my coat, but at last I reached dry land on a grassy hillock.

To my surprise I found that I was on the right track, for just below was unmistakably Blae Tarn. It is only a large pond, but yellow irises grew at one end, belying its name, which means the 'dark tarn', and four ducklings and some moorhens sailed across it as if it were a real lake. Here I picked up the Wall, with its ditch and the Vallum, again, the first two swerving a bit to the north. Crossing a field, I followed them along a pleasant lane for a mile and a half, the Vallum running some distance to the south through the fields. Here the weather brightened and the sun actually appeared long enough to cast shadows. At Wallhead poor old Hutton was received gloomily, he says, as he was mistaken for a surveyor sent by the landlord preparatory to raising the rent. Just before Walby the road deviates from the Wall to the north for a quarter of a mile. Here was Milecastle 62, but I could see nothing of it; the three previous milecastles have left no visible traces anyway. From here I took a lane which brought me out at Brunstock Park, through the grounds of which the course of the Wall could be faintly seen.

Here I ate an exiguous lunch and continued along the main road into Carlisle. The Wall's course could only be imagined among the suburban houses. It passes under a large military depot, appropriately named Hadrian's Camp, whose National Service men have, I was told, the best football team of its class in the country. Here a sudden spurt of rain drove me into a deserted and chilly inn, run on the 'Carlisle system', which seems to prefer hygiene to homeliness. When it cleared I walked on to Stanwix (pronounced with a silent 'w'), the northern suburb of Carlisle, where was the largest fort on the whole Wall.

This fort was well sited on a plateau halfway between two northern bends of the River Eden. Unfortunately there is nothing to be seen of it except its southern rampart in the churchyard. The Wall, which formed the north front of the fort, ran through the yard of the present school: the fort's southern wall ran just north of and roughly parallel to the Brampton Road: its eastern wall ran up Well Lane and its western passed just west of the church. The Vallum ran just south of the fort, but is not, as I at first thought, the ditch seen descending the hill east of the fort towards Well Lane. Stanwix is over eight miles from Castlesteads and covered nine and a third acres. Its name was Petriana and it housed the *ala Petriana*, a cavalry unit one thousand strong, the largest on the Wall. This was named after its founder, T. Pomponius Petra, and had been originally stationed at Corstopitum. One of the troopers is represented on his tombstone, now in Tullie House, Carlisle, horsed and equipped with spear and shield, trampling down a prostrate enemy. This was formerly in the wall of Old Stanwix church, where also was found a fine relief of Victory, with wings outspread and draperies agitated by her flight, now at Newcastle. Another tombstone from this fort was erected to Marcus Troianus Augustinus by his loving wife Aelia Ammillusima: his face is shown in a niche above the inscription, with a lion on each side, but the sculptor has adopted the untidy habit of starting lines with the last letters of the preceding lines. Another altar, found north of the fort, was erected to our old friend Cocidius, here equated with Mars, by two centuries of the Second Legion, the work being superintended by Oppius Felix, *optio* (deputy to a centurion).

From Stanwix I followed the presumed line of the Wall to the banks of the Eden and then took a bus to Carlisle and put up at the 'Red Lion' Hotel. Here I was more than ever glad of a bath after my adventures with mud and rain. I then visited the Museum at Tullie House, just beyond the Cathedral, where is another fine collection of Roman objects from many parts of Cumberland and useful reconstructions of the Wall and other Roman structures. Apparently the schools had just closed: anyway, the place was overrun by children who rushed yelling up and down the stairs and rioted among the show-cases with disgraceful disregard of more serious visitors. I suppose they thought it was a public place and so belonged to 'the people'.

Carlisle was an important Roman station a generation before the Wall was planned. Here Agricola (or possibly an earlier governor Petillius Cerialis, AD 71–4) built a fort and from here the Stanegate with its subsidiary forts set out on its journey eastwards to Corstopitum and perhaps beyond. Its name was Luguvallium, meaning the place of one Lugavalos, a name derived from a Celtic god called Lugus, who is at the root of the names of Lyon and Leiden. The Roman name was abbreviated to Luel by the Welsh, who prefixed Caer, meaning a Roman station, to give us the modern Carlisle. But little is known of its Roman days, since almost continuous settlement has persisted on the site and opportunities of excavation are now severely limited. Quite likely it was large enough to have a municipal council and some scholars think that St Patrick, whose father was a magistrate, came from here. In the seventh century St Cuthbert was taken by the citizens of the little town to see its fortifications and a fountain built in marvellous fashion by the Romans, but Bede, who tells us this, gives no details. It is known that the fort stood on the site of the Cathedral and that later a civil settlement grew up roughly within the limits of the medieval city. Excavations have unearthed traces of a timber stockade and of a large wooden platform, perhaps intended for a *ballistarium*, stone balls for which were found near by. Presumably, also, there was here a bridge over the Eden, similar to those farther east. The life of the settlement has to be reconstructed from the many monuments dug up and now at Tullie House.

One of the most interesting of these is a slab erected to Hercules by a native of Xanten on the Rhine to celebrate the rout of a vast horde of barbarians. This is thought to refer to the British war under Commodus at the end of the second century, in which southern Caledonia was lost. It must have been 'a famous victory', for the soldiers are called comrades of the god, on account of their valour (*ob virtutem*). Martial virtue is also celebrated on a slab to a Celtic god, Ocelus, here equated with Mars, and to the divinity of Alexander Severus and his mother Julia Mammaea. That admirable Emperor's name was erased after his death, as we have found elsewhere. A tombstone bears the pathetic legend DIS VACIA INFANS AN. III below a stiff representation of a small girl in a belted tunic and over-

cloak. A happier domestic incident appears to be hidden
under a laconic record that 'the father of Donatalis pays his
vow to the Fates', presumably a thankoffering for the son's
escape from some illness or other mischance. Then there is
a tombstone to Flavius Antigonus Papias, native of some
Greek city, who lived sixty years, more or less, at which
period he gave up his soul in resignation to fate. In spite of
the wording, the lettering suggests the probability that he
was a Christian: if so, it is one of the very few such found
near the Wall. Finally may be mentioned a fine large sepulchral slab, unfortunately uninscribed but dated to the second century, showing a woman sitting on a chair within a
shell-shaped vault resting on two pilasters. Her costume falls
in graceful folds about her: one hand holds a fan and the
other caresses a small boy, who plays with a bird in her lap.
The whole is surmounted by a sphinx and two lions devour-
ing a human head, as in the Stanwix monument mentioned
above, representing the ravages of death. One would give
much for details of this lady's history and some account of
her household. It is clear, at any rate, that security and
civilization had come to Carlisle, for such a monument
would have been impossible before the Romans came and
for many centuries after they left.

Tullie House contains many memorials from other places
in Cumberland. From Bewcastle come two more altars to
Cocidius, both erected by tribunes, one of whom was formerly a clerk to the Prefects of the Praetorian Guard at
Rome, the other an *evocatus*, or picked veteran. Then there
is one of a triad of Mother Goddesses, seated sedately in
ample Celtic dress falling in quite unclassical folds. An
altar to Jove from Maryport, set up by a native of the town
of Nimes in southern Gaul, and another to Maponus from
Old Penrith dedicated by two Germans illustrate, if further
illustration is necessary, the many races which jostled so
queerly along and around the Wall. Finally, an altar to
Jupiter and Vulcan erected by the village authorities (*vika-
norum magistri*) at Old Carlisle reminds us of the self-

government which even these small communities around the forts were permitted under the Roman constitution.

From Carlisle and Stanwix a Roman road led northwards to the outpost fort of Netherby on the River Esk, another of the 'eyes', like Bewcastle, of the Wall in the Cumberland sector where it was masked by hills to the north. It was called Castra Exploratorum, the scouts' camp. Nothing is now visible of this fort, but in 1725 Stukeley saw its foundations. He remarked that here 'is the most melancholy dreary view I ever beheld'. It was like 'the backdoor of creation; here and there a castellated house by the river, whither at night the cattle are all driven for security from the borderers. As for the houses of the cottagers, they are mean beyond imagination; most of mud and thatched with turf, without windows, only one storey; the people almost naked.' An inscription showed that the fort was built under Hadrian. There are several inscriptions from here at Tullie House. One records the building of a hall (*basilica*) for horse exercise under Alexander Severus. Another represents a genius, probably of the camp itself, naked to show his divinity, save for a most ineffectual mantle covering part of his legs, and a crown and high boots: one hand holds a cornucopia, the other a dish over an altar.

This road from Stanwix to Netherby is really a branch of a major Roman road which curves left to the fort of Birrens (Blatobulgium), near Ecclefechan. Built by Agricola, it underwent several reconstructions and appears to have been abandoned, like Netherby, in the mid-fourth century. Here were found a statue of Brigantia, the goddess of the Brigantes, winged and in long robes, holding spear and ball, made by Amandus *architectus* (we have met another of his calling at Chesters), and an altar to Minerva set up by the Second Cohort *equitata* of Tungrians, whom we have met at Castlesteads. For long this road was thought to end at Birrens, which was regarded as but one more outpost fort to the Wall, but recent excavations, assisted by air-photography, have shown that it was a trunk road into Caledonia, the western counterpart of Dere Street on the east. It ran up the valleys of the Nith and the upper Clyde to join Dere Street at Inveresk on the Forth and was crossed on the way by another road from Newstead on Dere Street running westwards down the Clyde valley to the western end of Antonine's Wall. It is now established that Agricola's advance into Caledonia was conducted up these two great military roads concurrently, to meet on the Forth estuary and thence combine for a grand push into the eastern coastal plain.

On leaving Tullie House it was so cold that I was forced to take refuge in a cinema. This is a relaxation I seldom indulge in and I can only say that I might have fared much worse. The main item was a Hollywood production dealing with the assault on Pearl Harbor. Here was one of the most dramatic incidents in the whole pageant of history, yet it was made the background to a trivial story of 'love' and regimental jealousy. The Japanese surprise onslaught was brilliantly done, but not an officer was on duty to take charge of the defences, and the panic-stricken troops were finally rallied by the hero, a sergeant. The younger females in the audience giggled at their antics, entirely unconscious of the tremendous import of this tragedy to humanity, including themselves. One wonders why a great nation presents its war exploits to the world in this sorry fashion.

After this it was some compensation to choose roast goose and fresh strawberries for dinner. I am usually fairly abstemious, but that night I felt I had deserved a treat. It was only afterwards that I remembered that it was Friday.

I had come to the last stage of my walk. I determined to reach Bowness on the morrow, come what might. So, to quote the sententious Sherlock, it was 'Early to bed, Watson, for I foresee that tomorrow may be an eventful day.'

13

CARLISLE TO BOWNESS

Heureux qui comme Ulysse a fait un beau voyage.
JOACHIM DU BELLAY

What was to prove my last day dawned hopefully. The sun shone brilliantly, but a high wind, driving swift ragged clouds up from the west, suggested that it was too fine to last. And it was cold enough for gloves, had I brought any with me. Before breakfast was over the rain started and quickly developed, not into the usual persistent downpour, but into a blinding, lashing fury that surely kept all sensible folk indoors. But nothing would stop me from at least essaying to finish my walk, bitterly disappointing as it was to have my last day spoiled in this wholesale fashion. So off I set, feeling as futile as on my first morning at Wallsend.

It was hopeless to try to follow the course of the Wall through the railway depot and sewage works just west of the Eden, where of course no traces of it are now visible. There was a bridge joining the Wall over the river here, and Camden saw 'within the channel of the river, mighty stones, the remains thereof'. One could wish that he had been a little more expansive in his accounts of this and some other remains which have vanished since his day, though we must be grateful that he took as much trouble as he did. He could not foresee the vandalism of succeeding generations. In fact, some heaps of stones from this bridge were recently found in the river-bed. So I tramped valiantly through the rain along the westward main road out of Carlisle, branching right at the church and on through the modern suburbs. On reaching open country I picked up the Wall ditch on the

right where it follows the south bank of the Eden just beyond the railway. Soon Wall and Vallum diverge considerably, the Wall clinging to the river to Grinsdale, the Vallum
running straight on to Kirkandrews. Before reaching the
latter, the two works approach again and run up the hill to
Beaumont (pronounced Beemunt). I diverged from the
main road to make this village, where I found the ditch well
marked as it climbed the hill from a burn. On the left of the
village street, about two yards from the top of the hill, part
of an inscription recording building by the Fifth Cohort of
the Twentieth Legion can be seen in a wall. On its right
side is a *pelta*, a common ornament on Roman monuments,
rather like the end of a turf-cutter.

At Beaumont the rain was so torrential that I sheltered
in the church porch for a time while gallons rolled off the
surrounding eaves. Near here, at Kirksteads, was found an
altar dedicated by the commander of the Sixth Legion to
celebrate victorious operations beyond the Wall (*ob res
trans vallum prospere gestas*), one of the few explicit memorials of engagements near the great barrier. We have just
noticed another such from Carlisle. We would give much
for more of these. It is a pity that the great mass of dedications did not record the events which gave rise to them.
Even these two are tantalizing in their brevity.

It was hopeless to wait for the rain to relent, so I set off
again along a lane running westwards behind the church
along the course of the Wall, which here makes a sharp turn
to the left away from the river. It is only a long mound,
which is all that we have seen of it since just past Castlesteads. This was a most unpleasant lane, full of ankle-deep
red mud looking like liquid chocolate, interspersed with
puddles and long wet grass. I at last escaped from this purgatory, only to be faced with the Powburgh Beck winding
over the flats, but eventually found a place where I could
jump it, instead of having to wade. Then I gained the road
to Burgh-by-Sands (pronounced Bruff). The exact course of
the Wall here is uncertain, but it is known to have joined

the line of the present road before reaching the fort.

This fort is five and a half miles from Stanwix and covered about five acres. Like many of the earlier forts its front (*praetentura*) projected beyond the Wall, so that the modern road runs roughly where the *via principalis* did. The church stands just to the south of this, in the usual place for the commandant's house, and is almost entirely built of stones from the fort. It is a lovely building, but one could wish that its creators had spared us a little of the Roman works. Very little excavation has been done here. An altar found at Beaumont and doubtless derived from Burgh, commemorates the *numerus* of Aurelian Moors, and as the *Notitia* places this unit at Aballaba (meaning apple orchard) this must have been the name of the fort. Other inscriptions show that it was garrisoned earlier by an *ala* of Tungrians and then by the First Cohort of Germans, It was large enough to hold a military cohort or an *ala* of five hundred men.

I found a few minutes' respite from the rain in the church, where the ladies of the village were busy with flowers for Sunday, but I was too rain-sodden to mar their work by lingering. So on through this pleasant village, with its variety of picturesque houses. It must be delightful in sunshine. At the newly-painted 'Greyhound' Inn, behind which the Vallum runs, I extricated myself from my wet garments and enjoyed a drink and some biscuits. Here a local man was being asked about the 'birthday party' at his house and replied that everything had gone well and that he had drowned all four. This startling announcement was presently explained when the mother, a nondescript bitch, appeared at the door in search of her murderous master. The latter told me that the Wall west of here ran out to the north of the main road by a large clump of gorse and then in an S-bend to the south at Dykesfield. He said that he had often dug up pieces of Roman pottery hereabouts and had once been lucky enough to find one of those small lamps produced in such quantities.

While we were talking a small miracle happened. The morning gloom was silently removed and presently sunlight shot through the windows. It seemed too good to be true, but so it was. My walk was to end in glorious sunshine from the bluest of skies, across which great white clouds sailed magnificently, reflecting and multiplying the light like gigantic mirrors. So, packing away my waterproofs, I stepped out across the bare marsh which opens west of the village. The road runs straight for nearly four miles, with the railway on the left. At ordinary times this would have been a monotonous stretch, but after the morning's disappointment, and with the end of my pilgrimage in sight, it was sheer joy. There was a fierce west wind, which often pulled me up short, but what did I care? Its challenge only spurred my strides. Whatever the weather, I was now sure of sunshine for the rest of the day.

To the right stretched the marsh in all its green flatness and, beyond, the silvery line of the Solway. It was here, on the July 7th, 1307, that Edward I breathed his last while waiting to cross the Firth to chastise the Scots, whom he had so often hammered but who somehow eluded complete conquest. I had visions of the proud medieval camp, bright with pennants and the flash of armour, peopling these lonely flats with unwonted animation, and of the dismayed murmurings when the news of the great king's death and of the craven abandonment of his designs by his unworthy son spread abroad. History never repeats itself, but it sometimes has a good try: here, for example, was a parallel to the death of another hammer of the Caledonians, Septimius Severus, at York in 211 and the winding up of his campaign by his sons Caracalla and Geta.

The road runs straight and flat to Drumburgh (pronounced Drumbruff), perched on a knoll. Here the railway ends, its last section to Bowness having been dismantled some years ago. The Wall is again visible ascending the hill to the village. Here was a small fort, four miles from Burgh-by-Sands. It is thought to be the Congavata of the *Notitia*, which stations the Second Cohort of Lingones there. Partial excavations in 1886, 1899 and since the last war showed that it was built after the turf wall, nearly two acres in extent, with clay ramparts, and that it was later rebuilt in stone, somewhat smaller. Its north side made square corners with the Wall like a milecastle but unlike the great majority of forts. For long the position of all the milecastles west of No 59 was rather conjectural, but recently No 76 was found one hundred and sixty yards east of Drumburgh, and the exact position of some others was ascertained.

On the left of the village street is Drumburgh Castle, cheek by jowl with humbler dwellings and conspicuous both by its antique air and by a sadly-weathered shield of arms. It was built under Henry VIII by Thomas, Lord Dacre, who stole most of his material from the Wall and the Roman station. It was too late to lament this vandalism, and I consoled myself with the panorama spread before me as I left the village and descended to the flats again. To the right was Solway Firth, fringed on the far side by the trim houses of Scottish villages, behind which rose range upon range of green hills. Far ahead were the peaks of Criffell, rising to nearly 1,900 feet, all like a miniature Snowdonia seen from the plains of Anglesey.

The wall is again visible on the left as one leaves Drumburgh. It accompanies the road as far as the school and then goes straight on across the fields to rejoin us farther on. It is only a green mound, but at places its stones can be seen, which is more than we have been vouchsafed for some miles. The road now reaches the coast for the first time and so continues to Bowness, curving to the right to Port Carlisle and then veering leftwards again, the Wall accompanying it on the left. It was very pleasant here. One feels one is at last right away from the busy world, for Bowness Common forms a promontory where no one comes unless he has business at the scattered farms. That day it certainly appeared 'a land in which it seemed always afternoon'. The attempt to make Port Carlisle a busy outlet to its greater namesake was a failure and the canal which was to have done what was later achieved at Manchester was drained and its channel used by the railway. And here at least the railway has yielded to the ubiquitous motorbus. So even this remote spot illustrates, in its successive works – Roman Wall, canal, railway and motor-road – the relentless march of history. Port Carlisle has a melancholy air, though facing a magnificent prospect – a row of staid Victorian houses, as if someone had started a miniature Ramsgate or Weymouth and grown tired, a disused jetty, but nothing pretentious enough to be picturesque in decay. Over the door of a house called Hesket, at a corner opposite a road running down to the sands, part of an altar to the Mother Goddesses is built into the wall: it is painted over in grey, but one can still make out MATRI in one line and BVS SVIS in the second.

I was helped in my search for this small relic by a farmer who had just alighted from his car near by. He kindly offered me a lift, and when I explained that I must walk, at least to Bowness, he showed me where I could find a good section of the Wall. It was about halfway between Port Carlisle and Bowness, through a gate on the left and perhaps two hundred yards from the road – a fine grassy bank some four feet high, with patches of stones and cement of the core showing up well. It was a poor thing in its way, after the miles of trim structures farther back, but I knew it was the last sight I should have of my Wall and I did not hurry away.

So I came to Bowness, the last fort and the end of Hadrian's Wall. There is little to see, for the modern village has covered most of the site, which was advantageously placed on a low headland. Its name was Maia and it covered some seven acres. It was thus the second largest Wall fort, after Stanwix, and housed a milliary cohort (one thousand foot nominal), but its garrisons are unknown. Like Housesteads, its long axis was parallel to the Wall. In the village street I again met my farmer friend, Mr Wills, now accompanied by the Rector, the Rev Norman Joyce, whose warden he told me he was. They showed me a small altar built into a stable on the south side of the main street, between the bus stop and the inn. It is in red stone and dedicated in ragged lettering by a tribune to Jupiter for the welfare of two ephemeral third-century Emperors. It is much weathered and will soon be unreadable if not protected. Also found here was a slab, now in Tullie House, containing part of a poem in which a suppliant, apparently some trader, vows to grace his verses with gilt lettering if the deity grants him a successful venture. On this, Mr E. B. Birley remarks that 'the dedicator must have been on the point of setting out on a trading voyage to the west of Scotland from the port at Bowness. No trace of gilding survives, so that we cannot be certain whether the voyage was a successful one.'

My companions then took me through the village and showed me where the western ditch of the fort can be seen running down to the shore between the body of the village and the school. Here the Wall continued past the fort into the water, as at Wallsend. 'I marvelled at first,' wrote Camden, 'why they built here so great fortifications, considering that for eight miles, or thereabouts, there lieth opposite a very great frith and arm of the sea; but now I understand, that at every ebb the water is so low, that the borderers and beast-stealers may easily wade over.' Beyond Bowness the Firth is not fordable and that was why the Roman engineers ended the Wall here. I dutifully went as far as I could in the direction indicated, though there are no remains now visible above water, so that I could say that I had followed the course of the Wall to its very end.

I was then taken to St Michael's Church, in the fabric of which are many Roman stones. The baths of the fort were found on the other side of the road from the church. Both my kindly companions offered me tea, but Mr Wills asserted his right as having met me first. I was certainly ready for it, after my long tramp, mostly on hard roads. So, entering a door inscribed 'W. M. W. 1699', for my host's ancestors had lived there for some three centuries, I joined a happy family party, after which Mr Wills showed me a box of Roman relics found on his land, including a complete mortarium with black gritty stones embedded in its bowl to help grind the food. Crusty old Hutton wrote 'I wished to converse with an intelligent resident [that is, on or near the Wall] but never saw one'; but everywhere I had found unfailing courtesy and much intelligent interest in my freakish enterprise.

And now my pilgrimage was over. *Veni, vidi, vici.* It was not much of a conquest, but it had several times threatened to turn into a 'wash-out'. On the whole, considering the kind of summer it was, I had been fortunate. Apart from the soakings on that first morning at Wallsend, at the end of my fourth day approaching Greatchesters and on this my last morning, I had had fine weather for my tour of the Wall itself. I certainly could not grumble. And now, as the bus hurried me back to Carlisle, eating up the miles which had taken so long on foot, the elements themselves seemed to join in my elation. Across the Solway the white houses of Annan stood out clearly in the sun as if they were only a mile away: behind rose the peaks of Criffell, and far away to the south-east the loftier outline of Skiddaw: while, above, pile upon pile of great white clouds with dark edges built up a fantastic celestial architecture, giving twice the sense of space that a clear sky would have done. From Criffell to Skiddaw was perhaps fifty miles, but this means nothing when one cannot see the intervening landscape. In the sky, however, by some trick of inverted geography, those fifty miles were expanded to a hundred.

On regaining Carlisle a bath was now more than ever welcome. How right the Romans were in this respect. By following their example I had never once felt stiff after my exertions. Nor had I suffered from foot troubles, apart from blisters the first day, when I unwisely wore two pairs of socks, following the advice of the experts. Never, I think, have I felt fitter than I did now, at the end of my tour. I felt as if I could tackle Everest, and kicked myself for deferring till now an experience which I might have enjoyed any time in the past forty years. I have always loved walking, but I owe my first real walking tour to Hadrian.

After dinner I enjoyed a pleasant English play at the local Repertory Theatre. Next morning was Sunday and I attended service in the magnificent Norman Cathedral, now, unhappily, but a fragment of its medieval vastness. It was good to find the Eucharist offered in the traditional English style and not in the borrowed rites dear to those enthusiasts whose motto seems to be 'Sweet are the uses of our adversaries'. So my pilgrimage, which started in the rainy gloom of Newcastle Cathedral, ended fittingly in the sunfilled glory of her western sister. Thence I went straight to the train for Euston. I had finished my course and to linger would only court an anticlimax. All the way down the sun shone in tune with my mood, for there is pardonable gratification at the achieving of any objective, however small. Yet, like Gibbon when he came to the end of his *Decline and Fall*, I knew there was something else. I had walked Hadrian's Wall, but I had left an old friend behind. I have revisited much of it since then, but I shall never again set out from Wallsend to explore the unknown all the way to Bowness.

Sestertius of Antoninus Pius, with Britannia on reverse

14

THE END OF THE WALL

And being done, thus Wall away doth go.
A Midsummer Night's Dream, v, i

We have followed our Wall to the end of its course, but not to the end of its history. Here and there we have hinted at its final fate, but if, as I hope, the reader has by now come to regard it as an old friend, he will doubtless be anxious to know, like little Peterkin, 'what became of it at last'. So I will try to satisfy his curiosity, though I must warn him that here we enter on dangerous ground.

For the end of the Wall is but one episode in the end of Roman Britain. And the period between the so-called departure of the Romans and the establishment of the English kingdoms is the darkest part of those Dark Ages which then ensued. Our authorities are so meagre, and they embody so much of myth and legend, that they afford a marvellous field, not only for the rival interpretations of acknowledged scholars, but for every sort of theory from inspired amateurs. I shall not try to follow the latter in any cut-and-dried solution of my own – for I am by no means inspired – but shall confine myself to indicating the few firm spots in this morass and the likeliest possible of the surrounding uncertainties.

Now this problem of the end of Roman Britain is itself but our own part of the general problem of the Decline and Fall of the whole Roman Empire. Here again historians are still arguing over its causes, though many phases of the problem are becoming fairly clear. One may perhaps hazard the guess that much of the mystery arises from posing the wrong question. For, as Gibbon pointed out, the problem is less Why did the Empire fall? than Why did it last so long? Nothing like this world-state has been seen, in the West at least, either before or since. It was in the nature of a miracle, created by extraordinary qualities in favourable circumstances and maintained by a happy equilibrium of forces which in the nature of things could not endure for ever. A once obscure city-state had conquered almost the whole known western world and had been endowed by Augustus with reorganized institutions designed to carry out its universal mission with fair efficiency. Its master and director was the *princeps*, who must be all-powerful, intelligent and ever vigilant: his agents were the upper middle class, which supplied the necessary brains, the leadership and the economic basis of the new order: below them was a prosperous *bourgeoisie* scattered throughout the Empire in flourishing cities: while an efficient permanent army maintained comparative peace. This régime attained its climax in the second century, in that golden age of the Antonines which Gibbon called the happiest in mankind's history. Under Emperors who saw themselves as the servants of their subjects, who were assisted by an efficient but not overgrown civil service, who kept taxation light and who left economic affairs to private initiative, a commonwealth of self-governing cities was established, throughout which scientific agriculture, inter-provincial trade and urban industries assured prosperity.

Unfortunately, Augustus had not solved all his problems. For this, of course, he is not to be blamed; but we can now discern some glaring defects in the Empire's condition which required remedying if disaster was to be averted.

First was the pressing problem of defence. Geographically, the Empire was but a fringe encircling an enormous inland sea, with a still more enormous land-frontier from which most of its great centres were not too safely distant. The west and south were protected by ocean and desert, but eastwards lay aggressive Persia, while all along the north were barbarians casting covetous eyes on its smiling countryside and wealthy cities. The army was absurdly small for the task which at any moment might confront it, for man-power was limited. It relied on its superior fighting qualities, but its armament differed only in degree, not in kind, from that of the barbarians. Massive retaliation was thus out of the question, and in fact the security of the Empire was staked on the inability of the barbarians to mount a concerted and continuous onslaught. If that came, survival would depend on whether the barbarians could retain and maintain what they were pretty certain to conquer. Logically, the solution here was to achieve natural frontiers by conquering the northern barbarians, but this was beyond the resources of the Empire, as Trajan's efforts had shown.

If this diagnosis is correct, it would be unnecessary to look further for the causes of Rome's fall. Some scholars, indeed, take this view. The Empire fell in the West, they say, because it was defeated in the field. Yet others argue that successful invasion was itself the result of internal decay. Certainly there were other factors at work. There was for instance the economic problem, which moreover had a direct bearing on that of defence. For the Empire could only be adequately defended if its economic power was intelligently harnessed to the exploitation of all its resources. And that, in the then state of economic knowledge, was impossible. The problem was not even envisaged.

Now the Roman economy was mainly agricultural and so incapable both of expansion and of being concentrated on the needs of defence. Though commerce flourished, industry was under-developed, for its market was restricted by the low purchasing power of the masses, a large minority of whom were slaves. The East had many thriving industrial centres and in time industries sprang up in other provinces, but this itself was largely the result of inadequate transport and remained merely a matter of local craftsmanship. The essential Roman despised trade and left it to freedmen and the lesser breeds. So fortunes were made in politics or commerce or speculation: savings were invested in land, less often in commerce. Under the early Empire a sort of feudal capitalism arose, but there was no development of large-scale industrial capitalism which alone, whatever its faults, could have extracted the utmost wealth from the Empire's natural resources. Consequently, as the late Professor Rostovtseff pointed out, the Empire's economy was not strong enough in the long run to maintain its political unity.

It is curious that, as practical people and as heirs to the remarkable achievements of all earlier ages, the Romans never lighted upon any of the great inventions which have transformed the world in the last few centuries. What might not have happened had their Empire been equipped with steam railways! So often they seem to have been on the verge of some great discovery, printing, for instance, but it failed to materialize and so the world slipped back to barbarism. Yet inventions would have come had there been any real demand for them and we must conclude that there was not. Some contend that slavery discouraged the development of machinery and the search for labour-saving devices. Others urge that slave-labour was expensive and that what hampered invention was the lack of cheap fuel. Yet the coal was there and was used to some extent. Slavery certainly had disastrous effects on education, science and medicine, and on the imperial administration, fields which were largely left to slaves and freedmen. The Romans could plan fine cities, fill them with grand buildings and link them by trunk roads. But they were more interested in Greek literature than in Greek science, they were bemused by a vapid rhetoric and left invention to the despised craftsmen. There was no conception of scientific progress, only a looking backwards to a golden age in the past.

A third factor in the Decline may be called the cultural. We must not think of the Empire as entirely populated by

Romans exuding pristine Latin virtues. Its eastern half was the home of a composite civilization embodying much older cultures – Egyptian, Chaldean, Syrian, Persian, but above all Greek, in its specifically later, attenuated, Hellenistic form. Now Greek civilization had long since passed its climax in the age of Pericles. The vigorous Roman genius had indeed produced a new state, succeeding in the political field where Greece had so conspicuously failed. But Rome had not created a new culture, she had only adapted that of Greece to her own genius. It was classical civilization that reigned throughout the Empire, a civilization of great value, but long since in decline.

This need not have spelled disaster, for it is not necessarily true that civilizations are born, flourish, decay and die. They are not men, they can be revived. But if, following Professor Toynbee, we attribute the rise of any civilization to a successful response to some great challenge on the part of a creative minority, which is able to enlist the cooperation of the less intelligent majority, then it must follow that it can only be kept at full pitch by eternal vigilance. Too often its leaders will acquire vested interests or be exploited by such: sometimes they may lose the support of the majority. Too often there will be mechanical imitation instead of continued creation: institutions once expressive of the first creative impulse will be idolized and become stereotyped, instead of being adapted to new circumstances. Too often there will be at best stagnation, at worst revolution. Continued creativity can only be maintained by a ruling class inspired by the highest intelligence and public spirit and able to evoke responsive cooperation from the rest of the community.

This was the problem which confronted the Roman Empire in the late second century. Its civilization was rich, but old; and it was spread over an enormous area among diverse peoples, many of whom had assimilated only a portion of its legacy. Given time, new creative impulses might have arisen, especially in the vigorous West; but time was not granted. At the end of the second century, and increasingly in the third, came the massed attacks of the barbarians so long dreaded, coupled with intermittent trouble from Persia. Everything had to be sacrificed to defence. This meant that all power had to be concentrated in the Emperor. Yet the constitution could not guarantee a good or wise emperor. Naturally, too, the engine of defence, the Army, acquired greater power and it soon discovered that it had no rivals and could make and unmake emperors at will. There followed a series of military revolutions which weakened and often disrupted the Empire while the barbarians were hammering at its gates. Salvation only came from a succession of vigorous emperors towards the end of the third century. Their work was crowned by Diocletian (284–305) and Constantine I (306–337), who stabilized the Empire by a thorough reorganization.

This reorganization both carried to their logical conclusion movements already afoot and introduced revolutionary features, creating almost a new society. Diocletian separated the civil and military administrations. The old provinces were replaced by larger dioceses, themselves subdivided into small provinces and grouped into four great prefectures. He practically doubled the army, which by Constantine's time was entirely remodelled. Legions and auxiliaries remained, but the main division was now between a mobile field army, ready to be dispatched to any threatened point, and frontier guards. Much greater use was made of cavalry and gradually static frontiers were replaced by defence in depth. The emperor had become an oriental despot, shrouded in awful majesty and served by an overgrown, all-powerful but corrupt and oppressive bureaucracy, aided by a secret police. Constantine also moved his capital from Rome to Constantinople, realizing that the West was more vulnerable than the East, a move which accentuated the always-present cleavage between a Greek eastern Empire and a Roman western one. He also, by his adoption of Christianity, gave the Empire a spiritual basis such as it had long been groping for. It is apparent how different was the Roman world of Constantine from that of Augustus.

It was different, too, in its social and economic complexion. The middle class, the backbone of the Antonine state, was not strong enough, in the absence of thorough industrialization, to provide the main basis of a world-monarchy, despite the emperors' encouragement of urban life everywhere. They clung to their privileged position, yet were largely content to remain mere *rentiers*. Hence the emperors became the tools of the army, now mainly a peasant force, which encouraged a policy favourable to the lower orders. So began a process of killing the goose that laid the golden eggs. Prosperity was already waning, what with the chaos produced by civil wars and the ever-mounting demands for defence: but now the state resorted to organized robbery in a desperate attempt to save itself. Men, money and supplies had to be obtained and quickly: so there must be all-round compulsion and any who resisted must be crushed. But if resistance was impossible, evasion was not, for an inefficient despotism can be bribed. So, while thousands were ruined, hundreds achieved a spurious wealth. These apart, prosperity naturally declined still further, until it almost vanished. The currency was continually debased, anyone who prospered was immediately penalized. Services to the state known as 'liturgies' and once willingly rendered by the bourgeoisie for the enrichment of their native towns, were made compulsory. Urban magistrates (*curiales*) were made responsible for taxes and liturgies, until their offices, charged with these burdens in perpetuity, became hereditary. The industrial classes were gradually enrolled in guilds, which they and their descendants were forbidden to desert. Since taxes in depreciated currency were insufficient, Diocletian turned the emergency requisitions in kind into a permanent levy on the land, thereby quickening the process which was transforming the small farmer into a *colonus*, a tenant whose position began to resemble that of the serf. The authorities seemed to find some peculiar magic in taxation, controls, compulsion and confiscation, but they were only trying to pull themselves up by their bootlaces.

Diocletian and Constantine, in fact, instead of copying Augustus in an intelligent reconstruction of the state, only perpetuated the emergency measures of the troublous third century. They secured a temporary success. The barbarian menace was removed, for the present: the economic activity of the state, now the largest owner of land and mines, and a large producer of some articles, was not ineffective. Yet the revival was only partial. The population had fallen considerably and some districts suffered from deforestation and soil-exhaustion. More fatal was the stifling of all enterprise and mobility, which led to a shrinkage of economic activity, except in luxuries, until inter-provincial trade almost ceased and every unit sought only self-sufficiency. The result was a gradual return to primitive methods and, except in a few districts, to bare subsistence, that is, to economic barbarism. The *laisser-faire* economy of the Augustan age had been replaced by a blind totalitarian polity, mercilessly grinding its subjects to death.

This economic and social revolution was part cause, but more symptom, of the Decline. The new totalitarian polity has been unfairly likened to both socialism and fascism, for it had no ideals but was adopted short-sightedly, step by step, as the only apparent salvation of the state. But what vitiated all endeavour in these disastrous centuries was the general failure of morale. The greatest achievement in statecraft of the ancient world, ruled by some of the most brilliant men in history, was slowly dying of barbarization and no one had the intelligence to arrest the process. Men had not lost faith in the Empire, but they lacked the will to preserve it. When the barbarians finally broke through its defences the whole Roman world held its breath, for the impossible had happened. Until then, men continued to boast with Claudian that Rome would rule the world for ever.

> Quod cuncti gens una sumus, nec terminus umquam
> Romanae dicionis erit . . .

But the old Roman spirit had gone. It might not have mattered that Roman blood had been swamped by provincials, by orientals, by the descendants of slaves and more recently by barbarians, for all these might have produced the necessary leaders. But supreme leaders do not arise full-armed out of nothing. They require a society in which education is valued, initiative rewarded and freedom of thought, speech and action is encouraged. But the economic revolution had destroyed the intelligentsia, penalized initiative, while encouraging greed, graft and oppression, and stifled freedom. First the popular assemblies, then the Senate, finally the cities, had lost their liberties; until political activity was quashed. There was no means of expressing public opinion and soon no public opinion to express. Everything had been sacrificed to the state, but the baby had been thrown out with the bath-water, leaving the state but a gigantic machine, without brains and without a soul. As there became less to control, and less power with which to exert control, society paradoxically moved slowly from the totalitarian state to the other extreme – feudalism – in which power, wealth and initiative were split among so many units that united action became increasingly difficult.

It might be thought that the groping towards a higher religion, culminating in the triumph of Christianity, would have supplied the will to survive. But the Christian gospel was other-worldly: it might inspire heroic action, but it could also induce resignation to temporal disaster. Here the state reaped the reward of its persecution, which had instilled a spirit of heroic resignation in Christians generally. Moreover, its official recognition had diluted the dynamic force of Christianity, and its triumph came too late to save the state. Pagans were as supine as Christians, for every-thing – the autocratic constitution, the destruction of the old intelligent ruling class, the dilution of the population by orientals bred to subservience, the economic barbarization – encouraged acquiescence.

And so we return to our starting-point. The creation of the Roman Empire was something of a miracle, but its preservation required an even greater miracle. That miracle was not forthcoming, because almost every condition for its happening was absent. Dr Gilbert Murray has recently felicitated Britain on possessing 'something very remark-able – a highly intelligent and competent middle class, doing the government of the country' (though he did not add that it is now being silently destroyed). It was this which the late Roman Empire lacked and which, I would venture to say, could alone have saved it. Instead, we find a militarized bureaucracy and an upper stratum of great landowners, misgoverning a population of impoverished townsmen, peasants, freedmen, slaves, dwindling industrial workers, idle city proletariats and infiltrating barbarians. A few saints, a few competent generals, a few bishops of elevated character, a few senators mindful of their high office, a few university professors – these could not save the Empire. So, while the East, based on Asia Minor and its impregnable capital, survived as a fossilized, oriental state, the West was overrun by the barbarians, whose irruption was less a spectacular Fall of the Empire than the logical conclusion to a long process.

The last chapter in the Decline of the West opened in the late fourth century. The death of Julian in a Persian war in 363 was followed by the division of the Empire between the brothers Valentinian I and Valens, under whom Goths, Alemans and Franks were with difficulty thrown back from the northern frontiers. Then the West Goths, driven for-ward by the Huns from Asia, crossed the Danube and de-feated and slew Valens on the fatal field of Adrianople in 378. The Empire, beset on so many sides, was saved by

Theodosius I, but on his death in 395 it was again divided, this time permanently, between his sons Arcadius and Honorius. As the fifth century opened the West Goths under their leader Alaric began persistent attacks on Italy which resulted in the capture of Rome itself in 410. A few years earlier Vandals, Alans and Suebi had swarmed across the Rhine to the Pyrenees, and then into Spain, while usurpers carved out transitory realms for themselves all over the West. In 412 the Goths moved into southern Gaul and later spread into Spain, from where, in 429, the Vandals crossed to Africa to establish an independent kingdom. Meanwhile the north-west fell under the sway of Aëtius, a Roman general who ruled as the half-acknowledged deputy of the western Emperor. It was he who combined with the Goths to foil the invasion of Attila and his Huns near Troyes in 451. Instinctively Romans and barbarians united to repel the Asiatic threat to Europe, but this done they reverted to their quarrels. In 476 the last of the puppet Emperors at Rome was deposed and the Western Empire dissolved into a congeries of barbarian kingdoms.

Naturally Britain shared this general decline of the Roman world. She was spared, it is true, the devastation of civil war. And as romanization was slighter here, she probably suffered less from the economic troubles that plagued the Continent so cruelly. Nevertheless there is clear evidence, at Wroxeter, Verulam, Caerwent, Silchester and elsewhere, of urban decline in the late third and fourth centuries. In contrast, the villas of the south and midlands were still functioning. Yet even here there was probably less efficient husbandry and declining production. Everything points to the increasing self-sufficiency of the villas, that is, to economic barbarization.

Britain's chief danger, however, was not internal decay but external attack. Not only were the Caledonians, now generally known as Picts, still rampant beyond the Wall, for the past century Scots from Ireland had been raiding the western coasts and had even made settlements in Wales. At the same time new raiders – Saxons, Franks and Frisians – had appeared in the English Channel and it had been necessary to create a new defence system in the south-east under a Count of the Saxon Shore. These measures were effective until the time of Julian, who had to send a field army to Britain to repel the inroads of the Picts and Scots. Then in 367 a great confederacy of barbarians was formed for a combined onslaught on the diocese. Picts, Scots and a people called Attacotti (probably a tribe just north of the Wall, levies from whom are found serving in the Roman armies elsewhere) swarmed across the Wall, part of whose garrison, described as the 'Arcani' (a name otherwise unknown, but probably indicating local levies employed to assist the auxiliaries as scouts), deserted to the invaders, and defeated and slew Fullofaudes, the 'Duke of the Britains' in charge of the frontier troops (*limitanei*) of the North. At the same time Nectaridus, Count of the Saxon Shore, perished at the hands of Saxons and Franks from overseas.

This was the most appalling disaster ever suffered by Roman arms in Britain, only possible through the unwonted combination of the enemy. Its traces along the Wall in destruction and burning, and in subsequent rebuilding, have already been noticed. They are especially visible at Chesters, Chesterholm, and Housesteads, the village outside which seems to have been abandoned as a result.

After sending over two generals who failed to retrieve these disasters, the emperor Valentinian I dispatched a tried soldier, Count Theodosius, who in the spring of 368 occupied London, but was held up by a mutiny and by the bands who ranged at will over the country. Theodosius therefore sent for expert assistants in the persons of Civilis, to restore the civil administration, and Dulcitius, to act as his second in command. He then gradually cleared the diocese of invaders and restored its cities, its northern garrisons and the Wall. His rebuilding is well attested all along the Wall, in rough but serviceable work, especially at Corbridge, Chesterholm, Birdoswald and Housesteads. But he did not restore the milecastles and turrets, a fact which may have been connected with his abolition of the untrustworthy Arcani, who had perhaps constituted the patrolling units of those structures. Nor did he restore the outpost forts north of the Wall. Birrens and High Rochester had not, as far as we know, been occupied since about 340: Bewcastle and Risingham had been rebuilt at some date before 367, but were not reoccupied thereafter, while Netherby certainly did not survive.

The poet Claudian celebrated Theodosius' victory in panegyrics which depict him pursuing Picts, Scots and Saxons across the northern ocean even to the Orkneys and Thule! This hyperbole may conceal some 'mopping up' expeditions against the discomfited barbarians. At all events Theodosius carried through a supremely thorough and successful rehabilitation of the distracted British diocese.

Ammianus Marcellinus, the historian who gives us the most detailed account of his work, adds a mysterious note which has a close bearing on the fate of the Wall. Theodosius, he says, recovered a province which he had previously lost to the enemy and so restored its former condition that it acquired a legitimate governor and was named Valentia by the Emperor, as if celebrating a triumph. This fifth province duly appears in the *Notitia Dignitatum*, but its whereabouts has long been a matter of controversy. Camden and many scholars since his day placed it in the Scottish Lowlands, between the two Walls; but Collingwood pointed out that this district had not been Roman territory for nearly two centuries, so that it could hardly be described as a province which Theodosius had lost to the enemy. Valentia, according to Collingwood, must have been those parts of Wales settled by the Scots. They must have been accepted by the government as allies (*foederati*) – a common practice in those days, by which barbarians who could not be expelled were given official recognition in the hope that they would eventually be absorbed. These Scots were now, he thought, deprived of this status and incor-

THE END OF THE WALL

porated into a fifth province under a regular governor.

Collingwood's thesis seems the likeliest, though it has been rejected by some scholars. Since Theodosius restored the Wall, it is unlikely that he ever thought of abandoning it, in which case Valentia cannot have been immediately to its south. It is just possible, of course, that in the early stages of this campaign things may have looked so black that he may have thought of surrendering northern England, but we have no hint of this and it seems almost unthinkable. This leaves the Lowlands and Wales as the only alternatives. And his abandonment of the forts north of the Wall seems conclusive against the Lowlands. Moreover, no late coins have been found there, except in the hoard at Traprain Law, such as we should expect if a province had been established there.

The invasion of 367 had a disastrous effect on the economy of the island. The towns, secure behind their walls, seem to have weathered the storm, but most of the villas seem to have been extinguished. Yet worse was to come. For in 383 Magnus Maximus, a prominent officer of Spanish birth in the British army, proclaimed himself Emperor against Valentinian's son Gratian. The usurper had served under Count Theodosius in the operations of 368–369, in which confused accounts in certain chronicles suggest he played a major part. If so, he may have resented Gratian's promotion of the younger Theodosius to high rank. One chronicler calls Maximus 'a vigorous and upright man worthy to be emperor', and it has even been suggested that he may have been the first governor of Valentia or alternatively commander of the frontier troops. His prominence in later Welsh legend shows that he had somehow impressed himself on the folk-memory of the West Britons. At all events, he determined to exploit the young Emperor's unpopularity with the legions and immediately crossed to Gaul, taking with him the cream of the British garrison. There he defeated Gratian, who was presently murdered, and soon made himself master of Gaul and Spain. But in

388, after winning Italy, he was defeated by the younger Theodosius, then Emperor of the East, and executed.

This continental adventure of Magnus Maximus is the key event in the mystery of the fate of Hadrian's Wall. For it has generally been held, at least for some forty years, that, in Collingwood's words, 'this was the end of the Wall'. The coins found on or near it, with a few exceptions which could be explained as the result of casual traffic, go down to 383, it was said, and then stop. Maximus, on this view, left a nucleus of troops to man the Saxon Shore, but withdrew those guarding Wales and the North. Thereupon, it was declared, the undefended Wall was once more overrun by the Picts and never reoccupied.

It is now clear that this account cannot stand, though as yet no certain substitute can be put in its place. If the reader finds this disappointing, he can console himself by trying his hand at the exciting piece of detective work which these maddening uncertainties invite, though he must not expect to reach a solution yet awhile.

In the first place, while it is true that Theodosius' restoration was the last rebuilding of the Wall, that need not mean that the reoccupation that followed lasted only fourteen years (369–383). It is by no means proved that the Wall was overrun in 383. At Birdoswald a barrack-block was looted and burnt soon after 375, but not necessarily after 383, and there are signs of burning at Chesterholm, but no indication of date. I prefer the opinion of the late Professor H. M. Chadwick that 'There seems to be no evidence for irruptions on a big scale after 367, though raiding took place locally'. Kipling, in his *Puck of Pook's Hill*, pictured the Wall as left by Maximus in charge of a suicide force, which was presently overwhelmed, but this is sheer conjecture. The destruction at Birdoswald and Chesterholm is just as likely to have been the work of local insurgents smarting under oppression and emboldened by the loosening of discipline in these latter days.

Secondly, it is not true that the coins on and about the

Wall go down to 383 and then stop. This is so at Wallsend and Benwell, but at Rudchester, Halton, Housesteads, Greatchesters and Carvoran the series ends earlier, at present. On the other hand, a coin of Valentinian II, dated between 389 and 392, was found at Chesterholm (where the Brigomaglos inscription clearly suggested a late civil settlement) and another of his at Chesters which appears to be latish and so after 383. Another from Castlesteads, very illegible, may be his or of Theodosius I (378–395). Coins of Arcadius (383 at earliest) have been found, one at Irthington and another at Birdoswald which is later than 389. South Shields produced one each of Arcadius and Honorius, the last not earlier than 393, Carlisle one of Honorius, Maryport a coin of 398–402 and Heddon-on-the-Wall one of 404–409. In addition to these isolated finds, a hoard from Corbridge contained thirteen of Magnus Maximus and Dr Kent has identified thirteen others from this centre covering the years 383–395. Finally, there is the hoard from Coventina's Well at Carrawburgh, which still awaits detailed examination but from which Dr Kent claims that five coins at least range from between 387 and 396. He therefore contends that the Wall garrison was not withdrawn by Maximus in 383: indeed, he argues that it would have been useless for an expeditionary force, being by that time composed of soldier-farmers who had been allotted lands in the neighbourhood on condition of performing garrison duties. We have to remember that the Roman armies had been remodelled at the end of the third century. Since then the mobile field armies had become partly barbarized but were still comparatively efficient, but the frontier troops (*limitanei*) had gone sadly to seed. We have already noted these farmer-soldiers at South Shields, where the fort was transformed in its last period into a sort of fortified village to house these hybrid troops and their families. We have vivid illustrations of this process from the Danubian frontier and from Africa.

This coin-evidence, even if it is slightly discounted to

allow for the enthusiasm of its advocates, cannot be brushed aside. Even were there no coins later than 383, Mr W. P. Hedley has argued forcibly that this would not prove that the Wall was then evacuated. At most forts we have so few coins from the fourth century that the absence from any particular fort of any after 383 is not by itself conclusive, for longer gaps can be found at earlier dates, when Wall and forts were in full commission. Also, all the late coins are much worn, suggesting that they saw long service. But with so many post-383 coins definitely attested, it is surely clear that many civil settlements, at least, on or near the Wall preserved some sort of existence for some time after Maximus left (which incidentally militates against any wholesale overrunning of the defences then). Could these settlements have persisted without protecting garrisons on the Wall, or at least in some of its forts? The answer may depend on whether any substitute was found which would maintain sufficient security, which I shall discuss later.

It may clear the air a little if we glance at the history of Roman Britain immediately after 383. It was some time after the death of Maximus before the agents of the Western Emperor were free to deal with Britain. Then Stilicho, the Vandal general to whom Theodosius I had entrusted his infant son Honorius, carried out the last great restoration of Roman rule in the island. Nearly all we know of his work comes from Claudian, who in poems written between 395 and 400 praises his hero for freeing Britain from Pict, Scot and Saxon. This suggests that until then the island was the prey of invaders, but too much must not be founded on these poetic outbursts, unsupported as they are by archaeology. In or about 402 Claudian tells us that Stilicho had to withdraw a legion from Britain to defend the nearer provinces, which has been identified with the Sixth Legion from York. Then came the swarming of the barbarians across the Rhine, whereupon the remaining troops in Britain (apparently the Second Legion, the Twentieth having probably been annihilated in 367) chose an Emperor of their own named Constantine to defend the island. The usurper, however, took most of his troops to Gaul in 407, to repeat the success and earn the ultimate fate of Maximus, Thereupon whatever authorities remained in Britain expelled his representatives and appealed to Honorius. That *fainéant* Emperor was in no position to help them and could only exhort them to look to their own safety.

This was in 410. Into the vexed question whether the Roman authorities ever recovered part of Britain thereafter we need not enter. But what was happening in the north, and particularly on the Wall? Besides the coin-evidence and Claudian we have only two sources to help us, both rather dim. There is also, of course, the account of Gildas, the sixth-century British ecclesiastic, but this can be ignored as confused and almost entirely unreliable. For he tells us that when, on the departure of Maximus, the Picts and Scots again attacked, the Romans sent a legion which built a turf wall across the island. On their withdrawal, the barbarians renewed their onslaught, whereupon the obliging Romans returned and built a stone wall. This likewise fell and the natives appealed in vain to Aëtius in or after 446. Desperate efforts have been made to torture some grain of truth out of this rigmarole. At best it seems to combine an account of the Saxon conquest with the author's ignorant surmises on the origin of the Wall. We can put it aside as nothing to our purpose.

To turn to our two other pieces of evidence, we have first the *Notitia Dignitatum*, a document either official or derived from official sources, listing the civil and military establishments of the Empire and dating, in its complete form, from about 430. Unfortunately, it contains various layers of information, compiled at different dates, which the 'higher critics' are still busy sorting out. Its British section includes a column headed '*Item per lineam valli*' ('Also, along the line of the Wall'), which names most of the forts on the Wall, as well as some in Cumberland, with their units. It is generally agreed that this list represents the situation long before the fifth century, and that it has somehow got 'frozen' instead of being kept up to date. For many of these units are shown in their third-century location and under antiquated titles. Why a more recent list was not drawn up still baffles the critics. If it had represented the garrison just before 383 it would have supported the alleged withdrawal by Maximus, since that would account for its never being revised: but as it is, it affords no help to the orthodox theory. Some scholars, indeed, think that the remainder of the British section of the *Notitia*, apart from *Per lineam valli*, represents Stilicho's reorganization of the northern frontier. It shows, it is said, that that general replaced the rigid wall-system by defence in depth, based on the military road north of York from Catterick to Carlisle. Such a withdrawal of the Wall garrison, about 396, would at least account for most of the post-383 coins so far found near it. But even this, if it happened, need not mean that the forts were thenceforward unoccupied.

For there is our second, even dimmer, source for this period. Later genealogies of Welsh princes include two which run back to chieftains of people called the Votadini and the Dumnonii, who in Roman times occupied the eastern and western portions respectively of the district between the two Walls. Several of these early chiefs have unmistakable Roman names, such as Aetern, Patern, Tacit, Cinhil (Quintilian) and Cluin (Clement). This suggests that their peoples had become partly romanized. Indeed, many scholars think they may have been adopted as Roman allies (*foederati*), charged with the defence of the frontiers. There is no actual proof of this, but the prominent part played by these two people in later history is best explained on some such theory. It is even suggested that Patern's nickname Pesrut ('red cloak') commemorates his investiture as captain of such an allied band of irregulars.

Unfortunately, scholars differ as to when this probable adoption occurred, one placing it in the third, another in the fourth century, others again ascribing it to Count Theodosius, Maximus or Stilicho. It is hardly likely to have been before the disaster of 367, for that would have shown the worthlessness of the expedient and these peoples would not be found collaborating with the authorities farther south thereafter. If Theodosius was its author, this might explain why he did not restore the forts beyond the Wall (it would also reinforce the arguments against placing Valentia north of it). If Maximus was responsible, this would support his alleged withdrawal of the Wall garrison, but this we have already seen is improbable. Its inauguration by Stilicho is more likely, since it would fit in with the coin-evidence and with the view that the *Notitia* reflects his rearrangement of the northern defences.

But what, it may be asked, were the Picts, so formidable in 367, doing all this time to allow these peoples to be established as Roman allies? The answer is that the Picts were not just beyond the Wall, ever ready to burst into Roman territory. Their home was behind the Forth–Clyde isthmus, though they may have had a settlement in Galloway. If two 'buffer states' could be successfully established between them and the Wall, the Picts might be effectively kept at bay. And this seems to have been what actually happened. We may envisage Maximus in 383 leaving the Wall garrisons, now reduced to a shadow of their old selves as mere soldier-farmers, in their forts, then Stilicho reinforcing them by allies beyond the Wall to fend off any Pictish attack. Whether the last-named withdrew the garrisons at the same time or whether they were allowed to remain until the allies farther north had proved their worth, we can only guess. If, as some think, the *Notitia* reflects the transfer of the British frontier forces to the continental field army, he probably did. Professor Richmond and Mr C. E. Stevens have suggested that the authorities may have established a local militia – a sort of Home Guard – to defend the military roads running north from York, whereabouts civil and military life was more prolonged and which was probably therefore the centre of the whole northern defensive system. If this were so, the same expedient may have been adopted on the Wall. The late Professor Charlesworth surmised that 'Henceforth, on the Wall, British troops, trained in Roman ways of fighting, and in the use of Roman weapons, were quite capable of defending their country'. In any case, if the northern allies proved their worth, as they seem to have done, the Wall garrisons would become unnecessary. Professor Richmond declared that 'Hadrian's Wall was not restored in AD 396 because its work was done'. Whether there was any formal withdrawal of the garrisons or whether, true to the practice of all old soldiers, they only faded away, does not greatly matter. Somehow, the time came when the work of the Wall was done and its structures were left to decline into ruins.

All this assumes that the Votadini and Dumnonii did the job supposedly entrusted to them. There are at least two reasons for such an assumption. Firstly, we hear no more of the Picts, apart from the unreliable Gildas, until 429, when they combined with the Saxons to raid Britain and were defeated by St Germanus. Secondly, we know that for some centuries a fairly stable British kingdom flourished in Strathclyde, that is, in south-west Scotland and Cumbria, whose kings traced their descent from the rulers of the Dumnonii. In the mid-fifth century the latter were ruled by a king called Coroticus, whose people were upbraided by St Patrick for raiding Ireland and enslaving some of his converts. It is to be noted that the saint tells his readers that this is not the conduct expected of Roman citizens. Nor, he adds, of Christians. For this district had been converted by St Ninian, a Romano-Briton whose career is unfortunately shrouded in obscurity. Ninian is said to have been consecrated bishop in Rome and to have returned to convert the southern Picts. We are also told that he built a church called Candida Casa (the White House) at Whithorn in Galloway. A twelfth-century writer adds that on his journey from Rome he visited St Martin at Tours, who died in 397 and to whom the church at Whithorn and several others in the area of Ninian's supposed labours were dedicated. This visit to St Martin is however rejected by most scholars, since it does not occur in any earlier account, and if they are right we have no certain date for Ninian. The dedications to St Martin must be later than 461, when his cult was started by the consecration of his basilica at Tours, so that they cannot be invoked. Nevertheless, Ninian's mission must have preceded Patrick's letter by at least a generation and was probably carried out a little before or after 400. If, as some think, it was contemporaneous with Stilicho's restoring work (who was himself a Christian), it would support the coin-evidence in suggesting that conditions were not too unsettled around the Wall and beyond, a consequence presumably of the establishment of the barbarian allies there. If the North were then being ravaged by Picts and Scots, Ninian's mission would have been unthinkable.

So also would have been the kingdom of Coroticus. Patrick, it may be noted, calls this king's soldiers *milites*, a term which suggests more than barbarian hordes: he also had Pictish and Scottish auxiliaries and possessed a fleet. It has been suggested that his kingdom owed much to the remnants of Roman institutions along the Wall. In any case, it looks as if the Dumnonii had carried out their office as *foederati* with sufficient success to remove the Pictish menace. This is borne out by a seventh-century source which relates that Cunedda, a chief of the Votadini and son or successor of the Aetern mentioned above, came from his home in Lothian with most of his tribe to north-west Wales, from which he expelled the Scottish settlers from Ireland. There is considerable controversy as to the date of his migration, but the better opinion places it about 450, when Coroticus was flourishing. This suggests that until then the Votadini were still guarding the eastern section of the lands north of the Wall, as were the Dumnonii their western part, and that they were so successful that the former could be detached for service in a more vulnerable area. The snag here is to account for the inroads of the Picts in 429 and later, but that is long after the Wall, on any theory, had been deserted, and need not trouble us here.

This, then, is the evidence as it stands today. If, greatly daring, I may hazard a tentative sketch of the picture which it presents to my mind, I would suggest the following. First, that when Magnus Maximus deserted Britain in 383 he probably left some sort of garrison on the Wall or in its forts. Secondly, that this may have been withdrawn by Stilicho about 396, when he reorganized the northern defence system. Thirdly, that that reorganization probably included the adoption of the two groups of lowland tribes, the Votadini and Dumnonii, as recognized allies and the establishment of local 'Home Guards' to assist defence. Fourthly, that in any case several civil settlements – South Shields, Corbridge, Chesterholm, Carrawburgh, Carlisle and Maryport at least – undoubtedly managed to survive for some time thereafter. Lastly, that the absence of complete anarchy in the North thus implied did not preclude considerable unrest, enough to account for the violent end which overtook South Shields, Chesterholm and some other places; but that generally speaking the civil and military centres there died of slow stagnation.

The reader will perhaps be disappointed at this rather tame conclusion. Surely, he will say, you need not be so wall-ridden that you must remain 'sitting on the wall' to the very end, waiting for something to turn up. But that is precisely the position. Nothing can justify a sure verdict where certainty is at present unattainable. Much more hard digging is necessary before the full story of the Wall's end is disclosed. If I can only, like Queen Elizabeth I, return 'an answer answerless', I must plead, with Luther, that 'I can no other'. I have at least given the reader some food for thought, and if he cares to follow up the work of the archaeologists as it proceeds he may have some of his questions answered. Some day, if the public, which showed such excitement over the London Mithraeum in 1954, will provide the necessary funds for the far more important work which cries out to be tackled up north, the Wall will reveal all its secrets. Meanwhile, we must 'wonder on, till truth makes all things plain.'

Solidus of Magnus Maximus, celebrating the 'victory of the Augusti'

INDEX

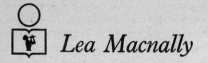

Lea Macnally